STRENGTH
SIGNIFICANCE. RESILIENCE. COURAGE.

Copyright © 2020 Hillsong International Ltd atf Hillsong International

Version 4

All rights reserved. No part of this book may be reproduced in any form by any mechanical or electronic means including information storage or retrieval systems, without permission in writing from the publisher.

While the manual is consistent with the values of Hillsong, the program and manual are suitable for use within any value or faith-based system. The purpose of this community development program is to promote a holistic, humanitarian and strengths-based approach to life.

Enquiries should be addressed to the publishers.

Hillsong Music Australia, PO Box 1195, Castle Hill NSW 1765, Australia

T: +61 2 8853 5300
F: +61 2 8846 4625
E: resources@hillsong.com

Warning:

The STRENGTH Facilitator Handbook and STRENGTH Journals are provided to help facilitate the running of the STRENGTH program. Although the content of the program is copyright protected it does NOT constitute, or contain legal, medical or other advice. Use of this handbook and running the program is entirely at your own risk.

Before running this program, you should obtain your own legal, insurance and other professional advice in the State, Territory or Country in which you intend to run the program.

STRENGTH
SIGNIFICANCE. RESILIENCE. COURAGE.

FACILITATOR HANDBOOK.

ACKNOWLEDGEMENTS
[WE WOULD LIKE TO ACKNOWLEDGE AND THANK THE FOLLOWING CONTRIBUTORS TO THE STRENGTH PROGRAM]

NICK KHIROYA	Pioneer Of Strength
KANE KEATINGE	Co-Pioneer of STRENGTH
RENEE YAM	M. Sexual Health, PGDipSocHlth, Cert IV TAA, B. Ec.
DR NANDILLA SPRY	DBA, M. Sd, BA, Cert IE TAE
CELINA MINA	M. Ed. (Int. Ed.), B. Ed., B. Arts, A. Mus. A.
SARAH MCMAHON	BA (Psych), PG Dip (Psych), Pg Dip (Psych Pr) Assoc MAPS
LYDIA JADE TURNER	BA (Psych) PG Dip (Psych) Assoc MAPS

Additional Contributions made by **DAVID KOBLER, TOMMY MCNAMARA, & LUKE PAA.**
Edits by **KATIE MAHER.**

We would like to thank **NICK KHIROYA** and **KANE KEATINGE** for making it possible to start this journey. Changing the world is a collaborative effort. Your commitment created many opportunities for young people all over the world to flourish.

FOREWORD

Helping adolescent men transition into manhood has been a concern all through human history. It was always given a lot of energy and care, and was something that the whole community got involved in. Eventually they knew everyone's lives depended on raising caring, safe and skilful young men.

We came close to losing the plot entirely on this - in the 20th century we experienced the most under-fathered generation of adolescent men ever raised. Through wars, recessions, the industrialisation of life, and people losing their sense of community, good men almost disappeared from the lives of adolescent men. This is why it's often dangerous to go out in the street after dark, and why we have suicide rates, divorce rates, crime rates, and accident rates like we do.

WE URGENTLY NEED GOOD MEN

Programs like this one that aim to give adolescent men a structured chance to think about what it means to be a good man, are much needed. They are a way to teach adolescent men how a real man acts to protect, care for and nurture the lives around him, and how he steps away from a focus on self to safeguarding all the life on the planet, at a time when it is so endangered.

This can be done without preaching, but by the sheer example of good men showing them, and taking time with them, and the chance to plumb down into their own hearts.

WARMEST WISHES TO EVERYONE WHO UNDERTAKES THIS WORK.

STEVE BIDDULPH

Steve Biddulph is the author of The New Manhood and Raising Adolescent Men. His books are in four million homes worldwide. He is an Adjunct Professor in the School of Psychology, Counselling at Cairnmillar Institute, Melbourne.

CONTENTS

INTRODUCTION .... *page 9*
STRENGTH OVERVIEW .... *page 12*
PROGRAM INFORMATION .... *page 15*
FOUNDATIONAL CONCEPT ONE: SIGNIFICANCE .... *page 38*
SESSION ONE: Leave Your Mark .... *page 41*
SESSION TWO: No Man is an Island .... *page 51*
FOUNDATIONAL CONCEPT TWO: RESILIENCE .... *page 60*
SESSION THREE: Can't Touch This .... *page 63*
SESSION FOUR: Too Tough to Get Rough .... *page 71*
SESSION FIVE: Power Balance .... *page 81*
FOUNDATIONAL CONCEPT THREE: COURAGE .... *page 90*
SESSION SIX: Too Traditional for Today .... *page 93*
SESSION SEVEN: Cause & Effect .... *page 103*
SESSION EIGHT: The Man for the Dream .... *page 113*
SESSION NINE: Live the Adventure .... *page 123*
APPENDICES .... *page 127*

STRENGTH
[INTRODUCTION]

INTRODUCTION

The STRENGTH program is about equipping adolescent men with the knowledge and skills to discover who they are and the person they want to become. It also encourages adolescent men to find the strength and courage within them to make healthy choices and live to their full potential. The program is not aimed at stereotyping what adolescent men should be like or how they should behave, but reinforcing that every person has different strengths, qualities and skills.

The STRENGTH program provides a new story of identity and is an opportunity for schools and teachers to demonstrate their commitment to the Quality Teaching Framework, School Leadership Capability Framework, Values Education Policy and Boys Education Policy. Additionally, this welfare-based program addresses syllabus outcomes from key learning areas such as from the Personal Development Health and Physical Education (PDHPE) curriculum, along with fostering literacy skills. The structure of STRENGTH enables schools and teachers to differentiate the content based on the individual learning needs of the participating students and can also be modified for the Life Skills curriculum or individual learning plans. The methodologies used are active participation and discussion forums. Therefore, such methods have been found to assist with social confidence, how to work with peers in a team or towards a goal, to speak up for themselves and to learn how to express emotions in a healthy manner.

Many young people in our communities do not know or believe they are valuable and unique individuals. Most struggle to find acceptance amongst their peers and genuine meaning for their life. A common mindset amongst young people is that 'If I am not of much value, then life doesn't have much purpose'. This inevitably creates a sense of living for the moment with little regard for consequences or the future. The impact of this 'meaninglessness of life' and loss of hope is made apparent by the fact that the youth suicide rate continues to increase not just in Australia but worldwide.[1] Lack of purpose instils negative mindsets in the lives of youth and can subsequently control the way they perceive their future. The break-up of the family unit, concerns of body image, coping with stress and young people believing they have little worth or nothing to contribute have far reaching implications – both immediate and long-term.[2] Research indicates that issues affecting male adolescents are largely neglected and are more serious than issues affecting female adolescence. Male participants have lower rates of literacy, grades, school engagement and a higher school dropout rate. Furthermore, the rate of arrests, suicides, injuries and premature deaths are higher.[3] STRENGTH aims to address these issues adolescent men may face and provide skills to navigate and overcome challenges through activities in a group environment.

---

1 World Health Organisation 2011, *Mental Health, Suicide prevention (SUPRE)*. [Online] Available: http://www.who.int/mental_health/prevention/suicide/suicideprevent/en/ [14/03/11]

2 Mission Australia, *National Survey of Young Australians 2010*. [Online] Available: www.missionaustralia.com.au/downloads/214-national-survey-of-young-australians [14/03/2011]

3 Robinson, J 2009, *New Study Shows Boys Face Serious Issues Which Are Being Ignored*, Medical News Today. [Online] Available: www.medicalnewstoday.com/articles/153152.php

STRENGTH OVERVIEW

STRENGTH is a unique personal development and group mentoring tool that uses an inspirational, practical and experiential approach to learning. This program is founded upon the premise that every life counts and has intrinsic value, and fosters an awareness of this belief. As a result, participants are equipped to become effective global citizens for the future.

AIM
For each participant to develop an understanding of the positive contribution they can make to the communities around them, and to know that they have **SIGNIFICANCE, RESILIENCE** and **COURAGE**.

OBJECTIVES
Equip participants to:

- Identify themselves as valuable with much to contribute.
- Build confidence, self-awareness and courage.
- Develop decision-making and problem-solving skills.
- Understand they are able to have a positive influence in their world.
- Identify personal strengths and desires to motivate them to set and achieve their goals.

THESE PROGRAM OBJECTIVES ARE ACHIEVED THROUGH 3 FOUNDATIONAL CONCEPTS: SIGNIFICANCE. RESILIENCE. COURAGE.

I HAVE

SIGNIFICANCE

BODY AND SOUL, I AM WONDERFULLY MADE The focus for these sessions is for each participant to learn that they have a significant role to play in building positive community with others, and to understand that they are valuable, unique and one-of-a-kind.

RESILIENCE

CHOOSE LIFE These sessions explore the power of choice and the impact that decisions have on shaping a person's future. This is addressed through practical sessions exploring resilience, respect, emotions, decision-making and problem-solving.

COURAGE

I HAVE A HOPE AND A FUTURE Being courageous is examined through exploring personal hopes, dreams, desires, attitudes towards relationships and risk-taking behaviours. Goal setting, group discussions and practical activities are used to explore these topics.

STRENGTH
[PROGRAM INFORMATION]

TARGET GROUP

STRENGTH is an adaptable program used in various local settings to reach high school boys in their 'middle years', generally this is from Grade 7 to Grade 10. The recommended group size for each STRENGTH program group is 8-15 participants. The program may be run in high schools, youth groups, youth centres, residential centres, community centres and juvenile detention centres. This program is not intended to replace the provision of formal case management, counselling or support for children and young people requiring professional assistance or intervention.

TEAM ROLES

Below are team roles that can be established for your program group. A minimum requirement to run a STRENGTH program is to have a Lead Facilitator.

FACILITATORS

LEAD FACILITATOR

The Lead Facilitator is responsible to lead and implement the STRENGTH program for a group of participants. The Lead Facilitator may or may not have a team working with them.

CO-FACILITATOR(S)

The Co-Facilitator(s) support the Lead Facilitator in running the program. Additional responsibilities include:

- Facilitating activities under the supervision of the Lead Facilitator.
- Having responsibility for a small group of participants within the larger program group e.g. leading the small group discussion segment of a session.

SUPPORT PERSONS

SPECIALIST SUPPORT PERSON

The Specialist Support Person comes alongside the facilitators and works specifically with participants who require extra care and assistance e.g. the School Counsellor.

The Specialist Support Person differs from the Co-Facilitator as they are working in the program with the purpose of assisting specific participants in the program group.

ASSISTANTS

Assistants give practical support to the facilitator(s). Assistants do not facilitate activities or lead small discussion groups. Assistant roles include:

- Set-up and room organisation.
- Helping set out the activity materials throughout the session.
- Assisting the participants practically (under the guidance of a facilitator) e.g. helping find a glue stick, and
- Clean-up.

Examples of an assistant include parent(s)/carer(s) and adult community volunteers.

RESOURCE CO-ORDINATOR

It can be very helpful for a STRENGTH program group to have a Resource Co-ordinator who can collect and put together the resources needed for each session. This role requires creativity and organisation. Having a Resource Co-ordinator is especially helpful when several STRENGTH programs are being run by an organisation. They can arrange for resources to be organised and/or purchased in bulk. A Resource Co-ordinator may also manage a team who assist the program groups with their resource requirements.

JUNIOR ASSISTANTS

Junior assistants fulfil the role of an assistant (as outlined above). An example of a Junior Assistant is a Peer Support Leader from the school where the STRENGTH program is being run. Junior assistants are to come under the definition of children and young people (refer to Child Well-Being and Safety, pp.17-27).

CHILD WELL-BEING & SAFETY

CHILD PROTECTION LEGISLATION

ORGANISATIONS ARE REQUIRED TO MEET LEGISLATIVE OBLIGATIONS IN RELATION TO CHILD PROTECTION. THEY ARE REQUIRED TO HAVE A CHILD PROTECTION POLICY THAT IS APPLICABLE TO THEIR COUNTRY, STATE OR TERRITORY.

Child protection legislation has been enacted by every state and territory of Australia. This legislation sets out legal and regulatory requirements around the interaction with children and young people, the care of children and young people, and the reporting of conduct of concern.

Facilitators and support persons are to be familiar with the organisation's policies and procedures that:

a) Guide staff and volunteers (i.e. facilitators and support persons) on how to relate to children and young people (i.e. participants and junior assistants).

b) Clarify the parameters of appropriate and inappropriate conduct for staff and volunteers (i.e. facilitators and support persons) to create a safe and supportive environment for the children and young people (i.e. participants and junior assistants).

c) Model a workplace that is collaborative, consultative and lawfully compliant in relation to current child protection practice.
d) Outline procedures for training and practice for staff and volunteers (i.e. facilitators and support persons) to fulfil their responsibilities:
   i) Under the specifications of legislation in terms of having a valid Working with Children's Check (WWCC)[1] (or equivalent standards of the country, state or territory where the STRENGTH program is run) and appropriate conduct.
   ii) To report inappropriate conduct directed towards children and young people.
   iiii) As Mandatory Reporters of concerns for children and young people at risk of significant harm.

---

[1] In New South Wales, Australia, before engaging a new, paid or volunteer, child-related worker, an organisation must ensure the worker has a clearance to work with children. The only way for an organisation to determine a person's clearance status is by verifying their WWCC with The Office of the Guardian.

CHILD WELL-BEING COORDINATOR

Organisations should designate a lead Child Well-Being Coordinator who is aware of all the STRENGTH programs that are occurring within their organisation. This person must be knowledgeable and experienced with child protection legislation for children and young people under the age of 18. They must be willing to be the key point of contact for all facilitators and support persons who will be involved in working with the children and young people participating in the STRENGTH program.

The Child Well-Being Coordinator must know the Child Well-Being requirements for their country, state or territory. They must prepare both the facilitators and support persons before each program is run and respond if there are concerns regarding child well-being and safety. In short, the coordinator must prevent and respond by:

- Coordinating processes to ensure all selected facilitators and support persons are safe and trusted adults.
  - Verify and record the status of the their WWCC (or equivalent standards of the country, state or territory where the STRENGTH program is run), and
  - Only engage child-related workers or eligible volunteers who have a valid WWCC.
  - Report findings of misconduct involving children and young people made against child-related workers or volunteers, and
  - Complete reference checks for facilitators and support persons.
- Ensure that the facilitators and support persons involved in the program have appropriate training.
- If there are concerns during the course of the program, implement policy and specific procedures e.g. identify, respond to and support children and young people when there are child well-being and safety risks and/or concerns.

DUTY OF CARE

All facilitators and support persons have a duty to take reasonable care for the safety and welfare of the children and young people (i.e. participants and junior assistants) in their care.

This duty is to consider and take all reasonable action to protect children and young people (i.e. participants and junior assistants) from known hazards or risk of harm that can be reasonably predicted. The standard of care that is required by a facilitator or a support person must take into consideration various factors, such as a child or young person's maturity and ability.

The duty of care responsibility for children and young people (i.e. participants and junior assistants) exercised by all facilitators and support persons applies during all activities and functions conducted or arranged by the organisation where a child or young person is in the care of facilitators and support persons.

The risk associated with any activity needs to be assessed and managed by facilitators and support persons before the activity is undertaken. A single serious failure to exercise appropriate duty of care, or persistent repeated failures, may constitute neglect or negligence according to the law if significant harm is caused or if there is the potential to cause significant harm to a child or young person (i.e. participant or junior assistant).

PERMISSIONS

Before a child or young person (i.e. participant or junior assistant) engages in the STRENGTH program, consent to participate is to be obtained from parent(s)/guardian(s) and/or the hosting organisation's contact person who is responsible for the children and young people e.g. in a school, it is the Principal.

Where a child or young person (i.e. participant or junior assistant) leaves the premises for an excursion (e.g. movie) or outing (e.g. going to a local sports oval to run a session activity), a permission slip for each child and young person is required to be signed by their parent/guardian. Where the program is run at a school, excursions or outings:

- Must first be approved by the school e.g. by the Principal.
- Permission slips are to be organised by the school contact, and
- Can only be run if a school staff member attends and has primary responsibility for the children.

PROFESSIONAL RELATIONS WITH PARTICIPANTS

All facilitators and support persons are to be caring and supportive adults who take an interest in the well-being of young people (i.e. participants and junior assistants), and who set appropriate boundaries for relations with children.

At all times, facilitators and support persons must treat children and young people (i.e. participants and junior assistants) with respect and behave in ways that promote their safety, welfare and well-being. Facilitators and support persons are always to act professionally. Your organisation's policies (that comply with the country state or territory's legislation where the STRENGTH program is run) will outline ways to assist facilitators and support persons maintain a correct professional relationship and boundaries with children and young people.

Where a small gift is provided to the participants during a session, the gift needs to be similar for each participant in the program group but may be customised for the individual e.g. if participants are each given a wooden alphabet letter the gift would customised by providing each participant with the letter of their first name or preferred name. There can be no differentiation in the quality or type of the gift as this can be viewed as favouritism.

Where a small gift is provided to each junior assistant to appreciate their time and contribution to the program group, the gift needs to be similar for each junior assistant but can be customised for the individual. The gift should be given on behalf of the STRENGTH program Group to the Junior Assistant. A good time to do this is in the last session.

CONFIDENTIALITY

It is important that all facilitators and support persons are aware of their confidentiality requirements. This means that discussions with community members about specific program groups or individuals are not allowed. Likewise, posting photos or comments about specific program groups or individuals on the Internet e.g. websites and social media, without consent is prohibited. Do not allow participants to take photographic or audio-visual material during the session.

Confidentiality does **not** extend to areas including:

- Mandatory reporting under child protection legislation. In a school in NSW Australia, mandatory reporting concerns must go directly to the principal and are not to be discussed with others e.g. team members, the classroom teacher or parent(s)/guardian(s). This will be outlined in the school's policies, however, this does not relieve the facilitator or support person from their obligation to be a mandatory reporter. For example, the seriousness of an allegation may warrant immediate contact with the police.
- When there is a serious threat to the life, health or safety to a person(s).
- Where program groups and/or individuals are discussed in the appropriate context e.g. communicating with your team, a child's parent/guardian or specific school staff about non-mandatory reporting issues.
- Where a signed and authorised use of image form is provided by the parent/guardian for audio visual, written or photographic material to be used from the participants e.g. on the organisation's promotional material, website or social media platform. Note: this is only applicable if it is compliant to the organisations policy e.g. a school may not permit photos to be taken at school events.

PRACTICAL GUIDELINES

Please note these are guidelines only. Team members are to follow their organisation's Child Well-Being and Safety policies that comply with their country and state or territory's legislation.

Please select one of the following applicable to your STRENGTH program group and read the corresponding information.

1. Facilitating the program at your venue, or
2. Facilitating the program where another organisation is hosting.

1. FACILITATING THE PROGRAM AT YOUR VENUE

COMMUNICATION WITH TEAM MEMBERS

- Identification must be worn by facilitators and support persons.
- Ensure facilitators and support persons have access to a phone in case of emergency.
- Team members are not to be alone with children and young people (i.e. participants and junior assistants) where they cannot be seen by others. Keep areas open with team members visible. For example, do not shut blinds or curtains in this situation.
- Do not initiate physical contact with children or young people (i.e. participants and junior assistants). When responding to appropriate physical contact initiated by younger participants, a shoulder hug, a pat on the back or a hand-hold are the only appropriate responses.
- Facilitators are to plan activities and responses are to be anticipated. If the participants become increasingly difficult to manage during an activity the Lead Facilitator is to stop the activity and regain management of the situation e.g. stop the activity and have the participants return to their desks.
- The Lead Facilitator is to have a key contact person's details who is available in case of emergency or where an immediate concern is identified e.g. a welfare officer. In a school in NSW Australia, if a reportable or potential reportable child protection matter arises, a person is required to tell the principal directly.
- Ensure the Lead Facilitator has the contact number(s) for each child and young person's (i.e. participants and junior assistants) parent(s)/guardian(s) and that these are kept current. It is advisable to have a secondary contact for each child and young person for use in case of emergency e.g. where the primary contact cannot be reached.
- Facilitators and support persons are to be fully aware of the venue protocols including:
  - Evacuation and lock down procedures.
  - First aid procedures, and
  - Location of bathrooms.
- Debrief with the team after each session e.g. What worked well? What can be improved? Are there any concerns about a child or young person? Are there any concerns about the venue? It is important concerns are documented and referrals made where needed.

COMMUNICATION WITH CHILDREN AND YOUNG PEOPLE
- Junior assistants are to come under the definition of children and young people.
- Children and young people (i.e. participants and junior assistants) are to go to bathrooms and/or other enclosed areas in groups and are not to go alone. Adult team members are not to be in the bathroom at the same time as children and young people.
- Children and young people (i.e. participants and junior assistants) need to be able to describe procedures for arriving and departing each session e.g. once their parent/guardian leaves them at the program they are to remain in the program until their parent/guardian returns and they are signed-out of the session.

COMMUNICATION WITH PARENT(S)/GUARDIAN(S)
- Intentionally communicate with parent(s)/guardian(s) about the program and their child's participation e.g. an information session, emails, SMS, posters/signs. Build relationships that are strong, positive and helpful.
- Determine a registration and dismissal process for the program. All children and young people (participants and junior assistants) should be signed in and out of each session.
- Communicate clearly and openly with parent(s)/guardian(s) around logistics for their child (i.e. participant or student volunteer) including the drop-off and pick-up time and location. Have a clear process for what happens if a:
  - Parent/guardian is late to collect their child.
  - Third-party will be collecting a child or young person from the program e.g. a family friend, or
  - A child is making their own way to and/or from the program e.g. using public transport.

NOTE ON FACILITATING THE PROGRAM AT YOUR VENUE:
Where the venue is a school and the Lead Facilitator is a school staff member e.g. a teacher, the person will already be aware of the school's policies and is to simply run the program within that framework.

2. FACILITATING THE PROGRAM WHERE ANOTHER ORGANISATION IS HOSTING

For a program being run in partnership with a hosting organisation, the guidelines below should be discussed e.g. with the key contact person in a school.

COMMUNICATION WITH TEAM MEMBERS:

- Identification must be worn by facilitators and support persons.
- Ensure that facilitators and support persons have access to a phone in case of emergency.
- Team members are not to be alone with children and young people (i.e. participants and junior assistants) where they cannot be seen by others. Keep areas open with team members visible. For example, do not shut blinds or curtains in this situation.
- Do not initiate physical contact with children or young people (i.e. participants and junior assistants). When responding to appropriate physical contact initiated by younger participants, a shoulder hug, a pat on the back or a hand-hold are the only appropriate responses.
- Facilitators are to plan activities and responses are to be anticipated. If the participants become increasingly difficult to manage during an activity the Lead Facilitator is to stop the activity and regain management of the situation e.g. stop the activity and have the participants return to their desks.
- The Lead Facilitator is to have a key contact person's details within the hosting organisation which is available in case of emergency or where an immediate concern is identified e.g. the classroom teacher. In a school in NSW Australia, if a reportable or potential reportable child protection matter arises, a person is required to tell the principal directly.
- Facilitators and support persons are to be fully aware of their hosting organisation and venue protocols including:
  - Evacuation and lock down procedures.
  - First aid procedures for the venue, and
  - Location of bathrooms.
- Debrief with the team after each session e.g. What worked well? What can be improved? Are there any concerns about a child or young person? Are there any concerns about the venue? It is important concerns are documented and referrals made where needed.

COMMUNICATION WITH CHILDREN AND YOUNG PEOPLE

- Junior assistants are to come under the definition of children and young people.
- Children and young people (i.e. participants and junior assistants) are to go to bathrooms and/or other enclosed areas in groups and are not to go alone. Adult team members are not to be in the bathroom at the same time as children and young people.
- Where a hosting organisation employee has not remained with the group e.g. the classroom teacher, participants need to be able to describe procedures for arriving and departing each session e.g. the Lead Facilitator will meet participants at their classroom; the classroom teacher will return at the end of the session, or the Lead Facilitators will take the participants to their designated playground area with the teacher on duty being advised that they have arrived.

COMMUNICATION WITH PARENT(S)/GUARDIAN(S) AND HOSTING ORGANISATION CONTACTS

- Intentionally communicate clearly and openly with the hosting organisation's key contacts e.g. principal, classroom teacher, school counsellor, about the program and the children and young persons' (i.e. participants and junior assistants) participation. Build relationships that are strong, positive and helpful.
- Discuss with the hosting organisation about the best way of intentionally communicating with parent(s)/guardian(s) about the program and their child's (i.e. participant or junior assistant) participation. Resources may be prepared by facilitator(s), however, **a key contact from the hosting organisation is to take on the responsibility of communicating directly with parent(s)/guardian(s).**
- Work with your hosting organisation contact e.g. classroom teacher, to determine a registration process for each child (i.e. participants and junior assistants). All children and young people should be signed in and out of each session.
- Have regular debriefs with your hosting organisation's key contact person.

ADDITIONAL REQUIREMENTS

A hosting organisation will generally require that all STRENGTH team members complete an induction and confirm that they have read and understood the material provided to them during their induction.

For example, a school may have all facilitator(s) and support person(s) complete an 'Acknowledgment by school community member' form or equivalent (applicable to your country, state or territory).

ACKNOWLEDGMENT BY SCHOOL COMMUNITY MEMBER:

I *(insert full name)* _____

Being engaged by the School in the following role *(insert position)* _____

Hereby acknowledge that I:

- Have received the Child Protection Policy and the School Code of Conduct for staff, students and volunteers.
- Have read the Child Protection Policy and the School Code of Conduct for staff, students and volunteers and am obliged to comply with the Code and Policy, including any amendments made by the School from time to time.
- Am obliged to notify the School if my Working With Children Check status changes from 'Cleared'.
- Am a Mandatory Reporter of concerns about children or young people being at risk of significant harm.
- Am obliged to inform the Principal of suspicion of reportable conduct of another community member.
- Have received training in all aspects of the Child Protection Policy.
- Am aware that a current copy of the Child Protection Code of Conduct and Child Protection Policy is posted on the School's website.

Signature	Date

OUTWORKING A SESSION

BRIEF
Allow time to brief your team on the plan for the session. Communication is vital for the team to operate well together. Make sure each team member knows what is required of them and that all tasks are delegated. Giving people responsibility means they are empowered to contribute. Participants can tell when a team is operating cohesively and when it is not.

BUDGET
Be creative with the budget you have. Recycle materials and, where possible, involve your community. Encourage people in your organisation, friends, family and community members to assist you in collecting recycled materials for use in session activities.

PREPARE
Preparation for a STRENGTH program takes time, organisation and thought. Every aspect of team member preparation can be used to create an atmosphere of value for participants. Where you intend to use music during a session, plan when the music will be played and at what volume. If you choose to use music with lyrics, listen carefully to the lyric before the session to ensure its suitability e.g. no explicit language or inappropriate content/references.

PRACTICAL TIPS FOR PREPARATION.
- Know your session content and program aims.
- Have the required resources for the session prepared in advance, and
- Have current knowledge of your Child Well-Being and Safety requirements for your group and venue (refer to Child Well-Being and Safety, pp. 17-27).

Being organised and mentally prepared will help each team member remain focused and present with their program group.

SET-UP

One of the key ways to demonstrate value to the participants is doing everything with excellence. Each session will require time to prepare resources and set-up the room. Ensure you arrive at your venue at least 20-minutes before you are due to start.

The presentation of the room can create a responsive, warm, friendly and open atmosphere and this is often the first thing the participants will encounter. Setting-up the room differently to regular classes or activities can create anticipation. It also shows that you believe the participants are worth the effort of arriving early and preparing the room nicely. This adds another layer to communicate value. Changing the room can increase learning capacity, create anticipation and lift expectations if done well.

Basic items can make a huge difference to the way the room looks. You can be as creative as you like but do not make it complicated. Simply placing the session title on the board can stir-up curiosity.

Always consider the needs of individual participants in your program group. You may have a participant who experiences some difficulty in the sensory environment such as a participant:

- Who may not be able to differentiate foreground from background noise.
- Where an increase in visual stimuli or a change to the room environment may result in sensory overstimulation.

For example, if working in a school, seek advice from the classroom teacher and/or the school counsellor.

PRACTICAL TIPS FOR SET-UP
- Keep the set-up design simple and modern.
- Make sure the room is safe, uncluttered and comfortable.
- Consider lighting, sound and positioning of furniture.
- Ensure the room set-up is conducive to effective class management.

IMPLEMENTATION

Give full attention and energy to your program group (this includes only using a mobile phone for emergencies). Here are some things to remember:

- Exude a friendly attitude
- Foster an environment where all participants can contribute
- Give clear directions and keep the group on task
- Draw out ideas and input from the group
- Actively listen to participants and other team members
- Be sensitive and non-judgemental
- Encourage the group to discover together
- Scaffold participants' learning

PARTICIPANT ASSESSMENT

The Lead Facilitator can use formative assessment, which is the process of gathering feedback during the sessions to assess if a participant is achieving the session outcomes. The teaching and learning activities are structured to enable the participants to achieve the outcomes. Formative assessment tools include the facilitator:

- Receiving informal feedback as a participant works through activities and contributes to group discussions, and
- Having each participant keep a portfolio of selected work from the sessions.

Where the program forms a part of an integrated unit of work in a school, the classroom teacher can put in place assessment tasks to further enable them to evaluate the effectiveness of the teaching and learning.

CLEAN-UP

Clean-up is an important part of running your program with excellence. Clean-up includes:

- Cleaning resources e.g. paintbrushes.
- Neatly packing away resources for use in future sessions e.g. posters, and
- Tidying and returning the room to the way it was (or better!).

DEBRIEF

Debriefing after each session allows the team to reflect and evaluate the session and prepare for the following week. Debriefing allows the team to identify what worked well and what can be improved upon and encourages personal reflection. If you have a specialist support person for your program, include them in this debrief. You may include assistants in the first part of the debrief but allow time for facilitator(s) and specialist support person(s) to have the opportunity to discuss any specific group concerns confidentially.

FOLLOW-UP

If you were asked a question during a session that you did not know the answer to:

- Make note of this (so you don't forget!)
- Research your response, and
- Plan your answer before the next session.

Where a concern is identified about a participant, follow your organisation's Child Well-Being and Safety policies that meet your country, state or territories requirements (refer to Child Well-Being and Safety, pp.17-27). Where a concern is identified about the venue, notify the person responsible.

SESSION OUTCOMES

Each session allows the participants to take part in an experiential and interactive activity and have the opportunity to socially interact and connect with the other participants and facilitators.

SIGNIFICANCE
By the end of this session each participant will be able to:

- **SESSION ONE: LEAVE YOUR MARK**
  Gain an understanding of the purpose of the program.
  Develop an awareness of personal value and identity.

- **SESSION TWO: NO MAN IS AN ISLAND**
  Explore the value of friendship.
  Discover the benefits of teamwork.

RESILIENCE
By the end of this session each participant will be able to:

- **SESSION THREE: CAN'T TOUCH THIS**
  Recognise the value of developing resilience.

- **SESSION FOUR: TOO TOUGH TO GET ROUGH**
  Identify healthy ways to display anger.
  Explore and understand that he is created with feelings.

- **SESSION FIVE: POWER BALANCE**
  Identify ways to display respect to others and themselves.

COURAGE
By the end of this session each participant will be able to:

- **SESSION SIX: TOO TRADITIONAL FOR TODAY**
  Develop understanding of a healthy relationship.
  Explore how to treat people with respect and dignity.

- **SESSION SEVEN: CAUSE & EFFECT**
  Gain understanding of the difference between healthy and unhealthy risk-taking.
  Identify consequences of healthy and unhealthy risk-taking.

- **SESSION EIGHT: THE MAN FOR THE DREAM**
  Recognise the importance of goal setting to achieve a dream or goal.
  Develop an understanding that he has something to contribute.

- **SESSION NINE: LIVE THE ADVENTURE**
  Describe what he has learnt from the program.
  Participate in a team building activity.

It is important to reinforce the foundational concepts throughout each session.

SESSION PLANS

The program is designed to be presented in nine 60-minute weekly sessions but can be adapted to other formats if necessary. In a school environment, it is usually conducted as one session per week during one or two high school teaching periods. The format is designed to enable the sessions to be adapted to other timeframes with ease.

The sessions are flexible in how they are delivered with regards to the order and style of presentation, however, it is recommended maintaining the program order where possible. As discussed earlier the key is to creatively express the specific concept each week and to create an environment where the participants have understanding about and experience the concepts presented.

Introduce the foundational concept at the beginning of each session, reinforcing it throughout and concluding each session with a brief overview of the concept by asking questions or giving the participants an opportunity to ask questions.

Each session's activities should relate to the 3 foundational concepts: Significance, Resilience and Courage. Each session has its own identified outcomes. Teamwork activities are incorporated into each session to build trust, a sense of belonging, interpersonal skills, collaboration and the opportunity to learn and grow from each other. The following teaching activities are the key components of each session:

- **Icebreaker:** Each session begins with an icebreaker ideally relevant to the concept. You can investigate the internet for alternative icebreakers and energisers. Icebreakers capture the attention of the group; the purpose is to 'break the ice' through a fun activity at the start of the session so that the participants are ready to receive, engage and get involved in the rest of the session.

- **Foundational concept:** This is used to open up and introduce the concept and topic. It's designed to be specific and sharp and can include definitions, brainstorming or illustrations.

- **Presentation:** This is the primary practical activity to achieve the outcomes. It is a chance for the group to understand and explore the concept being presented. Professionals can also be organised to present on the topic (recommended presenting time is 35 minutes).

- **Small group discussion:** Get the participants to break up into small groups for the last 5-10 minutes of every session. Where possible, the participants should stay in the same small group with the same facilitator for the entire program. Small groups are a great opportunity for the facilitator team to connect with each participant. This is a good opportunity to ask the participants questions that will help to summarise, recap and wrap up the session, encouraging them to share what they have learnt.

Note to the facilitator

As discussed before, the session topics are flexible in delivery. As the facilitator, it is vital you understand your group and the best way to deliver the topics in order to engage the group and draw them into the activity. Reading straight from the Facilitator Handbook to your group is not recommended. Use your own creativity and initiative to bring each topic to life, making it relevant to your target audience.

FOUNDATIONAL CONCEPT **ONE**

SIGNIFICANCE

SESSION ONE LEAVE YOUR MARK.
SESSION TWO NO MAN IS AN ISLAND.

BODY AND SOUL, I AM WONDERFULLY MADE

INTRODUCTION

SIG·NIF·I·CANCE *[SIG-NIF-I-KUHNS]* The quality of being worthy of attention; importance

U·NIQUE *[YOO-NEEK]* A one-off, original, exceptional, rare, unequalled, extraordinary, incomparable, matchless, individual

You are the only YOU there can BE. There is no one else like you. There is something in you that the world needs.

BE YOU...EVERYONE ELSE IS ALREADY TAKEN // AUTHOR UNKNOWN
WHY COMPARE YOURSELF WITH OTHERS? NO ONE IN THE ENTIRE WORLD CAN DO A BETTER JOB OF BEING YOU THAN YOU // AUTHOR UNKNOWN

Our lives are valuable, we are one-of-a-kind individuals and who we are is irreplaceable. There is a reason for our existence. We are not rubbish, we are not a mistake, and we are made with purpose.

Human life is valuable; it is the most precious commodity on earth. People's lives hold far greater value than fame or material wealth. An individual's value has nothing to do with what we think or what people say about us. Our value is not related to what we do and it is not based on our circumstance, family background, religion or how much money we have. Value can't be earned. Nothing can change how valuable we are. Because we are valuable, we are worthy of being treated well. This starts with us, valuing ourselves means looking after ourselves.

We are unique; there is no-one else the same as us. How we are designed, our passions, our talents, our strengths are unique to each of us and all have purpose. All these qualities are in us so we can fulfil our future; we are purpose-built and exist for a reason. There is a purpose for our lives.

What we do with our life is unique to our individual make-up. Our contribution to the world is significant because only we can make it. We can all do something and be someone of significance. We can leave our mark by making a positive contribution to the communities around us!

BODY AND SOUL, I AM WONDERFULLY MADE

1

SIGNIFICANCE
SESSION ONE LEAVE YOUR MARK

RECOMMENDED LAYOUT

MATERIAL REQUIRED: Strict rules game handout *(Appendix A)*; Butcher's paper; Coloured pens/permanent markers; Money note; Toy cars or picture of cars; Number plate handout *(Appendix B)*; Whiteboard and markers.

ACTIVITY	DETAILS	NOTES/MATERIALS
INTRODUCTION 10 mins	**ACTIVITY** Strict Rules Game Introduce the STRENGTH Program	Strict Rules Handout
ICEBREAKER 10 mins	**ACTIVITY** Introduce Yourself	
STRENGTH GUIDELINES 5 mins	Establish group guidelines	Butcher's paper; Markers
FOUNDATIONAL CONCEPT 10 mins	**YOU ARE SIGNIFICANT** **EXPLANATION** Famous Basketball Player	
PRESENTATION 20 mins	**DEMONSTRATION** Local currency note **ILLUSTRATION** Car **ACTIVITY** Signature **ACTIVITY** Number Plate	Butcher's paper; Coloured pens/permanent markers; Money note; Toy cars or picture of cars; Number plate handout; Whiteboard and markers.
SMALL GROUP DISCUSSION 5 mins	Q. What have you learnt about yourself today?	

NOTES

OUTCOMES
BY THE END OF THIS SESSION YOU WILL BE ABLE TO:
Gain an understanding of the purpose of the course.
Develop an awareness of personal value and identity.

INTRODUCTION
ACTIVITY: STRICT RULES GAME
Before the participants arrive for the first time, set the room up with a list of rules on each table. Ensure the rules are so strict that they could not possibly be achieved. As the participants arrive, tell them in an authoritative way to sit down promptly without talking. Read the rules out to the class without letting anyone interrupt you. After the rules have been read out, get every person to pick up the rules, rip them up and throw them away *(See Appendix A)*.

Explain to the group that this is not the way the group will be expected to behave. They will be included in the establishing the group guidelines for the group and will be treated with respect. This is also the way the facilitator will expect them to treat others in the group.

INTRODUCE YOURSELF
The facilitator and co-facilitator/s welcome the group and introduce themselves and share why they are there. Explain that you are volunteers and are not paid to be there but want to be. This is a great time to briefly refer to your experiences at school and how it would have benefited you to have 'older' guys coming in to share how to get the most out of school and life at their age.

Explain the program and briefly outline the program outcomes to the group in words the participants will understand. Build expectation.

Tell the group that you would like to be called by your first name, not 'Sir' or anything formal. Let the group know that even if you are running this class in a school, the STRENGTH program will not look like a class room and for them all to move the chairs and tables to the back of the room. After every STRENGTH session the chairs and tables need to be returned to where they were found.

ICEBREAKER
ACTIVITY: INTRODUCE YOURSELF

Get the participants to sit in a circle and encourage them to introduce themselves by telling everyone their favourite music, video game, class, sport, book, food etc. This is a great way of getting everyone to share about themselves.

When each participant gives an introduction, try and create a mini conversation with them. This helps establish rapport and trust as each individual is shown an interest in.

STRENGTH GUIDELINES

Establish Group Guidelines with the participants. You can do this by:

- Using your organisation or hosting organisations existing Group Guidelines (sometimes these will already be on a poster on the wall!)
- Collaborating with the participants to develop guidelines specific to that program group. Write these on a poster at the front of the room and bring them along to future sessions. Here is an example of Group Guidelines:
  - Arrive on time
  - Listen while others are speaking
  - Follow safety instructions
  - Mobile phones on silent and away
  - Stay calm
  - Be involved

When an individual participant needs a directive to correct poor behaviour, be clear and firm, without expressing anger. Where possible, speak to the participant quietly. If a situation is escalating or becomes unsafe, always ask for help from a supervisor or other adult team member. In a school context, seek immediate support from school staff.

FOUNDATIONAL CONCEPTS

> **Q. If you could be anyone, who would you be?**
> Ask the group to discuss ideas. The chances of anyone saying themselves are slim, and that is the point of the discussion. Why would you want to be anyone else other than you?

SIG·NIF·I·CANCE *[SIG-NIF-I-KUHNS]* The quality of being worthy of attention; importance.

U·NIQUE *[YOO-NEEK]* A one-off, original, exceptional, rare, unequalled, extraordinary, incomparable, matchless, individual.

Our lives are valuable. We are one-of-a-kind individuals. Who we are is irreplaceable. There is a reason for our existence. We are not rubbish. We are not a mistake. We are made with purpose.

Human life is valuable; it is the most precious commodity on earth. People's lives hold far greater value than fame or material wealth. An individual's value has nothing to do with what we think or what people say about us. Our value is not related to what we do and it is not based on our circumstances, family background, religion or how much money we have. Value can't be earned; nothing can change how valuable we are. Because we are valuable, we are worthy of being treated well and this starts with us, valuing ourselves means looking after ourselves.

We are unique; there is no-one else the same as us. How we are designed, our passions, our talents, our strengths are unique to each of us and have purpose. All these qualities are in us so we can fulfil our future. We are purpose-built and exist for a reason. There is a purpose for our lives.

YOU ARE THE ONLY YOU THERE CAN BE!

You are the only YOU there can BE. There is no one else like you. There is something in you that the world needs.

"BE YOU... EVERYONE ELSE IS ALREADY TAKEN" // AUTHOR UNKNOWN

"WHY COMPARE YOURSELF WITH OTHERS? NO ONE IN THE ENTIRE WORLD CAN DO A BETTER JOB OF BEING YOU THAN YOU" // AUTHOR UNKNOWN

EXPLANATION: FAMOUS BASKETBALL PLAYER

Michael Jordan is a worldwide famous basketball player. Imagine if when he was in school, football was the only acceptable 'cool' sport to play, and only a few people played basketball! Imagine if he didn't want to be different and just wanted to fit in with all the other football players. He would have spent his life being an average football player and not the gifted amazing basketball player he is now. He was true to his gifting.

PRESENTATION

DEMONSTRATION: LOCAL CURRENCY NOTE.
E.G. $5 OR $10

Here is a $10 note. What if I scrunched up this $10? What about if I stepped on it, crinkled it up and got it dirty? Would its value change?
No, its value remains the same even if it isn't treated with care. No matter what happens to you, whether you have been treated well or you have been mistreated. You have not lost your value. We are valuable and we remain valuable.

ILLUSTRATION: CAR
IF YOU WERE GIVEN A REALLY EXPENSIVE CAR

// How would you treat your new car?
// Where would you park it?
// Who would you let drive it?
// Would you drive it through rough terrain?
// Would you put premium petrol instead of normal unleaded petrol?
// Would you get it regularly serviced and cleaned?

HOW WE TREAT SOMETHING DEPENDS ON HOW VALUABLE WE THINK IT IS. EACH OF US IS PRICELESS AND EACH OF US IS OF HIGH WORTH AND VALUE. BECAUSE WE ARE VALUABLE, WE DESERVE TO BE TREATED WELL AND WITH RESPECT.

ACTIVITY: SIGNATURE

SIG·NA·TURE *[SIG-NUH-CHER, -CHOOR] One-of-a-kind style, personality, culture, heart, passion and vocation.*

Put a piece of butcher's paper in the middle of the table with permanent markers and coloured pencils. Ask the participants to write their signature down anywhere on the paper. This activity could be stretched into drawing a certain picture or graffiti writing, depending on what is most suitable for your target group.

Once everyone has completed their signature, ask the participants to stand back and look at all the drawings. Emphasise the difference in handwriting and signatures. No signature is the same.

Everyone has a different way of expressing their signature. This signature is an expression of their personal style and their creativity. We are all responsible for bringing out the signature message in us.

ACTIVITY: NUMBER PLATE

Come up with a 6-letter acronym for your number plate that represents you *(See Appendix B)*.

Each and every one of us has a different life story, upbringing or background and we may even speak different languages. Lots of things in our society pressure us to fit in and conform, to be part of the crowd and not stand out. However, we are all unique with different gifts and talents that only we can bring to the world. We are all designed to stand out and be unique individuals. Conforming to the status quo, peers, or culture does not help us step into our purpose.

SMALL GROUP DISCUSSION

Q. What have you learnt about yourself today?
Take some time this week to think about what you like to do and why you like doing it. For example, if you like football, why do you like it? It could be that you enjoy comradery. This is part of the discovery of your personal identity.

NOTES

BODY AND SOUL, I AM WONDERFULLY MADE

2
SIGNIFICANCE
SESSION TWO NO MAN IS AN ISLAND

RECOMMENDED LAYOUT

MATERIAL REQUIRED: Friendship quiz handout *(Appendix C)*; Tent pole; Pens; Whiteboard and whiteboard markers; Tables & chairs; Blindfolds.

ACTIVITY	DETAILS	NOTES/MATERIALS
ICEBREAKER 10 mins	**ACTIVITY** Catch and Throw	
FOUNDATIONAL CONCEPT 10 mins	**SIGNIFICANCE**	
PRESENTATION 35 mins	Friendships & Peer Influencing **GROUP DISCUSSION** Friendships **ACTIVITY** Friendship Quiz **TEAMWORK ACTIVITY** Tent Pole	Friendship quiz handout, tent pole.
SMALL GROUP DISCUSSION 5 mins	Q. What can you do practically this week to develop friendships? Q. What did you like about working in a team today?	

NOTES

OUTCOMES
BY THE END OF THIS SESSION YOU WILL BE ABLE TO:
Explore the value of friendship.
Discover the benefits of teamwork.

ICEBREAKER
ACTIVITY: CATCH AND THROW
Form a circle not too far away, but close enough to throw a ball to each other. The person who has the ball goes first by saying their name and then saying the name of the person in their group who they will throw the ball to (underarm throw). Once they have said the name of the person they will throw the ball to, they throw the ball. The second person says their name and the name of the person who they will throw the ball to. Once the group has gone around once, get them to do this activity faster. The key is for everyone to be alert and ready to catch the ball.

FOUNDATIONAL CONCEPT
SIG·NIF·I·CANCE *[SIG-NIF-I-KUHNS]* The quality of being worthy of attention; importance
U·NIQUE *[YOO-NEEK]* A one-off, original, exceptional, rare, unequalled, extraordinary, incomparable, matchless, individual

Reiterate this again: we are unique; there is no one else who is the same as us. How we are designed, our passions, our talents, and our strengths are unique to each of us and have purpose. All these qualities are in us so we can fulfil our future. We are purpose-built and exist for a reason. There is a purpose for our lives. What we do with our life is unique to our individual make-up. Our contribution to the world is significant because only we can make it. We can all do something and be someone of significance.

HOW CAN YOU BE YOU?
- Be confident that you can contribute
- Stand-up for what is right
- Put yourself out there, try new things, and discover what gifts are in you

PRESENTATION
FRIENDSHIPS

Friends will shape our future, and surrounding ourselves with friends that encourage us to make right choices are worth the time and effort, because 'no man is an island'.

Friendship is vital in a young person's life and can set a platform for their future. Friendship contributes to how a young person makes decisions, changes how they view themselves and either hinders or helps develop many of the social skills they will carry into their adult life. Young people need positive influences around them. Peer pressure can cause young people to conform to behaviours they perceive as acceptable by their friends. Friends have a large role to play in influencing young people's lives.

We are not meant to do life alone. Life is a partnership with people, friends and family and we are wired for relationship. The best thing about life is not what you do, but who you get to do it with. Steve Biddulph quotes in his book *'The New Manhood'*, "Male friendships give you courage, humour and strength to do more in the world."[17]

PEER INFLUENCING

Our friends and the people in our world can influence us to do well or not so well in our lives. We can also live to be our best or our worst because of the influence we allow our friends to have on us. We all need each other; therefore it's important to choose our friends wisely.

Who are we allowing to influence our life? What type of influence does each friend have on us? Does their friendship draw out the best or worst in us? Do they encourage to make right or wrong choices.

Friendship can be explained like a castle. Every castle has a moat and the only way in or out of the castle is through a drawbridge. The drawbridge will only be opened to outsiders with the permission of the gatekeeper — which is you. We should look at friendships this way.

---

[17] Extracts from *The New Manhood: The handbook for a new kind of man* by Steve Biddulph are copyright of the author and are reproduced with the permission of Finch Publishing, Sydney.

GROUP DISCUSSION: FRIENDSHIPS

Q. What is a friend?
This question will help the facilitator to gain an understanding of what the participants depict a friend to be. Possible responses may be: someone to hang with, I don't have any friends, someone with similar interests, or someone who sticks up for you.

Q. Why do I need friends?
Possible responses may be: So we can encourage each other when things get tough, we can work together as a great team, to help me not feel lonely.

Q. What do you value in friendship? What qualities make a good friend? What do these qualities practically look like in a friendship?
Possible responses may be: trust, loyalty, fun, encouragement.

The key is to highlight the qualities that the group have said they value and encourage them to be that type of friend to others. The facilitator can also suggest the following qualities which the participants may not have mentioned:

- Friends that will 'sharpen' you (i.e. challenge you, push you forward, and tell you what you may not want to hear but do so because they have your best interests at heart). Friends that can listen to you, give you constructive advice.

Q. What friendships are important for your future?
This question will encourage the participants to explore how friendships will shape their future. Young guys don't need to limit their friendships to their classroom, local community or sporting team. They can be friends to people that are different in age and location. Explore the thought about having friends important to your future.

- Have you ever done anything you wouldn't have normally done, that had a positive impact, because of a friend?

Q. How can friends influence us?
Encourage the participants to talk about the positive and negative influences that friendships can have. Highlight to the group that they don't need to wait for the type of friends they want in their life to come along; they can start to be that type of friend to others now.

Furthermore, highlight the benefit of having role models or mentors in a young person's life and how they can help a young person in a positive way.

ACTIVITY: FRIENDSHIP QUIZ

Distribute the quiz to each participant to fill out. Participants can choose more than one response for each question. Once the quiz is completed, collect the quizzes and get your co-facilitator to look through the answers. Find the main responses for each situation and discuss with the group why they chose that response. The key is to highlight throughout these discussions what a good friend looks like in real-life scenarios. *(See Appendix C.)*

1. A kid in your class has been having a hard time with some guys in your grade who are picking on him. What do you do?
- ☐ Sit back and watch them bully him. You're glad it's not you.
- ☐ Stand up for him and report it to the teacher.
- ☐ Befriend him and invite him into your circle of friends.

2. Your friend is a star football player. He is regarded by his peers as someone everyone wants to be like. Colleges are coming to your school to scout players they can offer scholarships to. He has told you that he will be taking steroids so he can look bigger and stand out to the scouts. What do you?
- ☐ Talk him out of it by giving advice on the health risks and what could happen if he gets caught (he could get drug tested, lose his reputation and not be offered a place at college.)
- ☐ Tell him to go for it. It's worth taking the risk, and you don't want him to succeed.
- ☐ Don't say anything; it's his free choice.
- ☐ Tell someone because it's illegal.

3. Your friend is going through a hard time. After a bad day, he tells you he wants to drink alcohol to forget about his problems. What do you do?
- ☐ Join him. Any excuse to drink is great for you.
- ☐ Offer an alternative activity you could do together that would cheer him up. You know that drinking is not really going to help him deal with his problems.

4. Your friend has told you he's being beaten up at school but he doesn't want you to tell anyone. What do you do?

- ☐ Say nothing. You respect your friend's decision even though you're concerned about him.
- ☐ Report it to the teacher or trusted adult who you think can help him.
- ☐ Tell a friend.

5. You have formed friendships with a great crew of guys. They always have your back and never pay you out. You are out with your friends on the weekend hanging out at the local shops. Your friends see this guy walking past who they don't like and start beating him up. You pull back as you don't want to be a part of it. Your friends tell you that you have to be involved and if you want them to be loyal to you, you have to be loyal to them. What do you do?

- ☐ Get involved in the fight, you don't want them to come after you next time.
- ☐ Tell them you don't agree with this and walk away.
- ☐ Report it to someone in authority.

TEAMWORK

Break the group up into 2 smaller groups. Explain that this will be their team for all teamwork and group activities throughout the STRENGTH sessions. This will help build teamwork, trust, loyalty and camaraderie throughout the STRENGTH program.

The best way to grow is together, learning from each other. The atmosphere that is created in the teams will affect the level of success the team will have. We can all bring different strengths to achieve an overall goal. The key is to draw on each other's strengths to get the best outcome, and together everyone wins.

**"THE STRENGTH OF THE TEAM IS EACH INDIVIDUAL MEMBER;
THE STRENGTH OF EACH MEMBER IS THE TEAM."** // AUTHOR UNKNOWN

ACTIVITY: TENT POLE

EQUIPMENT
Tent pole (a pole that unfolds into a tent pole) or helium stick.

PROCEDURE
- Get the participants to form 2 lines facing each other.
- Have the participants raise their arms to chest height, pointing their index finger out to the person opposite them.
- Lay the tent pole across all the fingers. The participants need to adjust their finger heights until the tent pole is horizontal and everyone's index finger is touching the pole.
- Explain the challenge to the participants: to lower the pole to the ground without anyone's fingers leaving the pole. The pole must rest on top of everyone's index fingers; pinching or grabbing the pole is not allowed.
- If anyone's finger is not touching the pole, they have to start the game again.

NOTES TO FACILITATOR

Ensure that you conclude the game only when the participants have completed the objective of the game. Even if it takes an extended period of time, the participants will gain more once they have completed the objective. There will be a great sense of accomplishment for the students and a real readiness for them to listen and find out why it took so long to accomplish the task.

- Act surprised when you see the pole being raised rather than being lowered. The collective pressure from everyone's fingers tends to be greater than the weight of the pole. Therefore, the more the group tries, the more the pole tends to be raised.
- Discuss the group's initial reaction to the game.
- Discuss how the group thought they handled the challenge; what skills did it take to be successful, what solutions were suggested and how were they received?
- Discuss the strengths and weaknesses of the group from an observer's perspective.
- Discuss with the group what each member learnt about themselves.
- Conclude the discussion summarising the purpose of the game: we all need others to achieve a common goal. Each person played a different role but each role is significant and important. We all need to learn how to work together with others, particularly people who are different to us (e.g. personality style).
- Explain that the more each individual works together in STRENGTH, the more each individual will get out of this program overall. We all need each other to participate because a great way to learn is from each other.

SMALL GROUP DISCUSSION

Q. What can you do practically this week to develop friendships?
Q. What did you like about working in a team today?

FOUNDATIONAL CONCEPT **TWO**

RESILIENCE

SESSION THREE CAN'T TOUCH THIS.
SESSION FOUR TOO TOUGH TO GET ROUGH.
SESSION FIVE POWER BALANCE.

CHOOSE LIFE

INTRODUCTION
RE·SIL·IENCE *[RI-ZIL-YUHNS, -ZIL-EE-UHNS]* Ability to recover readily from adversity

Resilience is the strength to withstand adversity; it is the ability to handle difficult situations, people, environments and setbacks. It helps in overcoming life's challenges, temptations and adversity. Being able to bounce back and recover from adversity make us stronger and contributes to our dreams becoming a reality. Young people can have incredible resilience. They can continually surprise us with their ability to bounce back rather than giving in to circumstances.

A resilient person is able to stand firm whilst facing significant difficulties and stress, as they have a strong sense of faith in their capabilities.

We need to understand that life will not always be smooth sailing and is not always great. Things happen that we would prefer didn't. But if life was always wonderful, would we appreciate all the great things or would we take them for granted? We can learn so much about ourselves when we go through challenges and problems. It is never comfortable when you're in the middle of adversity or challenge, but as you work through it you can look back and see what you have learnt from the situations.

DECISIONS WE MAKE DON'T JUST AFFECT OUR LIFE; THEY ALL IMPACT THE PEOPLE AROUND US. CHOICES CAN BE SELFISH OR SELFLESS. EVERY DECISION WE MAKE HAS A CONSEQUENCE. OFTEN WE DON'T REALISE THAT IT'S THE SMALL, EVERYDAY DECISIONS THAT CAN HAVE A PROFOUND IMPACT ON OUR FUTURE.

CHOOSE LIFE

RECOMMENDED LAYOUT

MATERIAL REQUIRED: Chopsticks; Soft ball; Jellybeans; DVD for movie scene; Bowls; Personal reflection handout *(Appendix D)*; Paper, coloured pens/pencils; Whiteboard & whiteboard markers; **For additional Activity:** Music; Lyrics.

ACTIVITY	DETAILS	NOTES/MATERIALS
ICEBREAKER 10 mins	**ACTIVITY** Chopsticks Game	Chopsticks, jelly beans, bowls
FOUNDATIONAL CONCEPT 10 mins	**RESILIENCE**	
PRESENTATION 35 mins	**DEMONSTRATION** Movie Scene **GROUP DISCUSSION** Resilience in Young People **DEMONSTRATION** Throw a ball **ACTIVITY** Personal Reflection **ACTIVITY** Testimony	Ball, personal reflection handout
SMALL GROUP DISCUSSION 5 mins	Q. What have you learnt today that you can apply to your life this week?	

NOTES

OUTCOMES
BY THE END OF THIS SESSION YOU WILL BE ABLE TO:
Recognise the value of developing resilience.

ICEBREAKER
ACTIVITY: CHOPSTICKS GAME
Split the group up into their teams. Give each student a bowl with some jellybeans in it and a set of chopsticks. No one is to eat the jellybeans until the game starts. Explain the instructions of the game: each student has to try and eat the jellybeans using chopsticks only, **no hands.**

This game will take some time for the students to finish and will test their patience, willpower and resilience. Take note of the different reactions everyone has to the game. This activity may bring many things to the surface to talk about during group discussion. Keep an eye out for the participants who lose their patience and give up and the participants who persevered through the game until they ate all their jellybeans. The team that finishes first wins.

Be aware of participants who have special dietary requirements and are not able to play the game. Ensure those participants are still included in the activity. For example, you could give them the role of team referee.

FOUNDATIONAL CONCEPT... RESILIENCE
RE·SIL·IENCE *[RI-ZIL-YUHNS, -ZIL-EE-UHNS]* Ability to recover readily from adversity

Resilience is the strength to withstand adversity. It is the ability to handle difficult situations, people, environments and setbacks. It is the key to overcoming life's challenges, temptations and adversity. Being able to bounce back and recover from adversity makes us stronger and contributes to our dreams becoming a reality. Young people can have incredible resilience. They can continually surprise us with their ability to bounce back rather than giving in to circumstances.

A resilient person is able to stand firm whilst facing significant difficulties and stress, as they have a strong sense of faith in their capabilities.

We need to understand that life will not always be smooth sailing. Life is not always great. Things happen that we would prefer didn't. But if life was always wonderful, would we appreciate all the great things or would we take them for granted? We can learn so much about ourselves when we go through challenges and problems. It is never comfortable when you're in the middle of adversity or challenge, but as you work through it you can look back and see what you have learnt from the situation.

PRESENTATION
DEMONSTRATION: MOVIE SCENE
Choose a movie that displays a character that has overcome adversity and developed resilience. Show a few scenes that display their experience of adversity and resilience to explain this concept further. The following are suggested movies that relate to resilience: *The Pursuit of Happyness, The Blind Side* and *Racing Stripes*. Note: Ensure the movie is appropriate for the age of the participants in your group.

GROUP DISCUSSION: RESILIENCE IN YOUNG PEOPLE
Q. What are some challenges young people face every day?
- Peer pressure
- Losing a loved one
- Bullying
- Rejection
- Negative self-talk
- Loneliness
- Addictions & substance use
- Parents separating/getting divorced

Q. How can you increase your resilience?
- Developing healthy relationships
- Learning from your failures
- Participating in new activities
- Getting information to understand what you're facing
- Talking to a trusted adult
- Being open to try again
- Overcoming problems, not giving up
- Adapting to new situations easily
- Standing up for what is right
- Being honest about your fears
- Taking healthy risks
- Facing rejection or setbacks and trying again
- Persevering when things get tough
- Not taking things personally
- Spending time with people who handle stress well.

Q. What are some things that can make it hard to overcome challenges?
- Isolation
- Negativity
- Boredom
- Indifference

DEMONSTRATION: THROW A BALL

Get two volunteers to come to the front of the class. Have one of them throw a soft ball to the other (underarm throw). His first reaction would be to catch the ball. Often our first instance is to accept the experiences that have happened to us and allow them to become part of our identity.

WE ALL HAVE THE CHOICE TO EITHER ACCEPT OR OVERCOME ADVERSITY, TO ACT OR REACT TO OUR SITUATIONS.

Now have the participant fold his arms and when a soft ball is thrown to him allow it to bounce off him. He exercised the power of choice and allowed the ball to roll off him. We can choose our responses to our situations.

Note: To keep this activity safe, **do not** use a ball that is hard.

ACTIVITY: PERSONAL REFLECTION – *(see Appendix D)*

Distribute a piece of paper and pen for each individual:

Write down a list of positive achievements you have accomplished and a list of difficult experiences you have overcome.

Encourage the group to spend some time writing down their answers. Tell the participants that they will not be asked to share their response with the group and they can take their worksheets with them at the end of the session.

After they have done this, bring the class back together and ask if anyone wants to volunteer to share what they have written. Explore what the participants gained from persevering. Use this to build and encourage the group to stay motivated when facing difficult situations. As the facilitator, be prepared to start the discussion off first.

ACTIVITY: TESTIMONY

Bring in a guest to share their testimony of overcoming and developing resilience in their life. Ensure their testimony is suitable for your specific program group e.g. age and maturity of participants. To make it as successful as possible, bring in a guest who may have a story that relates to the participants in your class. If you are unable to invite an appropriate guest, use a clip from a movie which you think could be relevant.

Encourage the group that if and when they face tough challenges in their life, it's important to talk about it with trusted adult. Planning and problem-solving challenges can help us overcome. We are not designed to do life alone. We need each other.

SMALL GROUP DISCUSSION
Q. What have you learnt today that you can apply to your life this week?

CHOOSE LIFE

4
RESILIENCE
SESSION FOUR TOO TOUGH TO GET ROUGH

RECOMMENDED LAYOUT

MATERIAL REQUIRED: Vocation picture; Feelings cards *(Appendix E)*; Balloons; Whiteboard & whiteboard markers.

ACTIVITY	DETAILS	NOTES/MATERIALS
ICEBREAKER 10 mins	**ACTIVITY** Contributing	Vocation pictures
FOUNDATIONAL CONCEPT 10 mins	**RESILIENCE**	
PRESENTATION 35 mins	**ACTIVITY** Balloon Control **ACTIVITY** Feeling Cards **ILLUSTRATION** Set the Scene	Balloons, Feeling Cards
SMALL GROUP DISCUSSION 5 mins	Q. What are some ways you can remain calm even when you are feeling angry?	

NOTES

OUTCOMES
BY THE END OF THIS SESSION YOU WILL BE ABLE TO:
Understand anger and why we feel it.
Identify healthy ways to display anger.

ICEBREAKER
ACTIVITY: CONTRIBUTING
Find pictures (e.g. from magazines, stock images) of men in their vocation. Ensure you have pictures of men from different ages and cultures, and include both paid and voluntary roles. Examples include emergency services personnel, mechanic, home carer, architect, chef, actor, engineer, teacher, chef, allied health professional, sports player and shop attendant.

Distribute the pictures to the participants and discuss the following questions:

Q. What work is the man doing?
Q. How are they making a contribution to their community?

Explore the concept

> **"MEN USE THEIR STRENGTH TO SERVE OTHERS"**

Q. What are some ways you can make a positive contribution in your community?

FOUNDATIONAL CONCEPT

RE·SIL·IENCE *[RI-ZIL-YUHNS, -ZIL-EE-UHNS]* The ability to return to the original position or form after being compressed, bent, or stretched.

Q. How do you understand resilience?
Q. What are some areas in life you've had to display resilience (being dropped from the football team, failing an exam, moving house)?

No matter what happens in life, whether we feel powerless or not, we have the power of choice.
We have the choice to: **RESPOND** to a situation or **REACT** to it.

This session is about managing your anger. When you get mad, **you have a choice** *and you can express it in a healthy manner.*

PRESENTATION
ACTIVITY: BALLOON CONTROL
Give each participant 2 balloons. Get them to blow up the first balloon to the point where it bursts. Then ask them to blow up the second balloon as big as it can get without bursting and then slowly deflate it.
This activity can illustrate how we have a choice to positively manage our emotions. We can make wise and helpful choices and express our emotions in a healthy manner or to make a choice to let them get the better of you.

ANGER
Anger is a frequently misunderstood emotion. It is often seen as unhealthy, destructive and unhelpful. Well-managed anger can be a useful emotion that motivates us to make positive changes and can help us identify where there is a hurt that needs to be addressed. Alternatively, suppressed anger may lead to depression and violence.

ACTIVITY: FEELINGS CARDS

Prepare a set of 'feelings' cards *(see Appendix E)*.

Give out cards with different emotions on them. The participants then need to categorise the emotions on the cards under the headings:
ANGRY, HAPPY, SAD, FEARFUL, COMBINATION.

PRIMARY FEELINGS	ANGRY	HAPPY	SAD	FEARFUL	COMBINATION
EMOTIONS	Furious	Excited	Grief	Nervous	Guilty
	Irritated	Satisfied	Miserable	Terrified	Jealous
	Annoyed	Pleased	Down	Anxious	Shame
	Ticked off	Joyful	Disappointed	Worried	Embarrassed
	Humiliated	Delighted	Hurt	Concerned	Uncomfortable
	Frustrated	Comfortable	Lonely	Afraid	Confused
	Hurt	Hopeful	Forgotten	Uncertain	Torn
	Sarcastic	Surprised	Remorseful	Out of control	Envious
	Disgusted	Positive	Rejected	Uneasy	Compassion

What we feel can generally fall under these 5 categories. A feeling that falls under the 'combination' category means that the feeling consists of a number of feelings. For example, embarrassed can be a combination of angry and fearful. You are probably angry about the position you are in and fearful that you might make a mistake.

Explain to the group that other, helpful words can be used to describe anger. For instance, an embarrassing situation could lead to a person feeling angry. If they understand the cause of their emotion (embarrassment) they will be better equipped to deal with their feelings of anger.

Put all the cards with different emotions on the floor. Then ask each participant to pick a card that explains what they are feeling now.

Q. How do we deal with anger?
On a physical level, anger prepares the body to either run from a potentially threatening situation or to stay and fight.

SOME SIGNS OF ANGER
- We can shake, get hot and sweat.
- Our muscles get tense. We may clench our jaws or fists and feel tightness in our chest.
- Our breathing gets faster and we may experience an upset feeling in our stomach.
- We may experience mental signs including loss of concentration, irritability, confusion, memory problems and a short temper.

THERE ARE THREE STEPS TO DEAL WITH THE EMOTION OF ANGER

1. Identify that you are getting angry:
- How do you know when you are angry?
- What was the point at which you were aware of your anger?
- Where in your body do you feel anger? List the physical signs of being angry.

2. Use a distraction strategy:
- Count backwards from 100 in multiples of 2, to calm down.
- Listen to calm, soothing music, or music that you enjoy.
- Engage in activities that you enjoy; play games, watch TV, read a book, or walk to the store. Take your mind off the situation.
- Exercise: go outdoors for a walk/run or play a sport you enjoy with friends.

3. Develop a problem-focused strategy:
- Get away from the situation; to think and reflect.
- Talk to a trusted adult such as a parent or local helpline number.
- Write down a list of your feelings. Express your anger on paper and calm down before working through the situation .
- Make a plan to deal with the trigger points, the early stages of your anger.
- Learn new ways of dealing positively with your anger. Practice these until they become habits.

ILLUSTRATION: SET THE SCENE

A kick boxer entered a pub and went to buy a beer. On his way back from the bar he accidentally bumped into a guy and spilt his beer. The guy was intoxicated and was really annoyed that his beer was spilt. He started picking a fight with the kick boxer, swearing and throwing punches at him. The kick boxer was trying to calm him down by apologising and offering to buy him another beer.

Q. Who do you think is the stronger person?
Q. What are some healthy ways of dealing with anger?

Encourage the participants to share with the group and put their answers on the board.

Unhealthy anger can cause harm to others or ourselves, such as violence.

SMALL GROUP DISCUSSION

Q. What are some ways you can remain calm even when you are feeling angry?

Encourage the participants to share with the group and put their answers on the board.

To conclude this session, encourage the participants to think of a trusted adult they can talk to about things that are really important to them such as dealing with the anger they feel. If they don't have anyone in their world they can talk to, offer the phone number of a youth helpline where they can call anonymously to talk to someone in confidence, or make a referal to a qualified professional e.g. the school counsellor.

NOTES

NOTES

CHOOSE LIFE

5
RESILIENCE
SESSION FIVE POWER BALANCE

RECOMMENDED LAYOUT

MATERIAL REQUIRED: Bar of chocolate; A pair of Chopsticks; Dice; Tape; Whiteboard & whiteboard markers.

ACTIVITY	DETAILS	NOTES/MATERIALS
ICEBREAKER 10 mins	**ACTIVITY** Chocolate Game	Chocolate bar, Chopsticks, Dice
FOUNDATIONAL CONCEPT 10 mins	**RESILIENCE**	
PRESENTATION 35 mins	**RESPECT** **GROUP DISCUSSION** Respect **ACTIVITY** The Line Game **DISCUSSION** Bullying & Cyber-bullying	Tape
SMALL GROUP DISCUSSION 5 mins	Q. What can you do to display respect to yourself, your peers, your teachers or your family this week?	

NOTES

OUTCOMES
BY THE END OF THIS SESSION YOU WILL BE ABLE TO:
Identify ways to display respect to others and themselves.

ICEBREAKER
ACTIVITY: CHOCOLATE GAME
- Sit the group in a circle or split the group up into their teams.
  Place a chocolate bar in the middle of the circle on a plate with a pair of chopsticks and a dice.
- Go around the circle rolling the dice.
- When someone rolls a 6, they get to break off a piece of chocolate with the chopsticks, and eat it.

Note: They break the chocolate off with the chopsticks, but take if from the plate with their fingers, to eat it. Have them break off only one piece at a time.

- Whilst this is happening, the rest of the group continue to try to roll a 6.
- Once the next person rolls a 6, the person eating the chocolate must stop, hand the chopsticks over, and the next person tries to break off a piece of the chocolate.
- The game continues until all the chocolate is eaten.

Note: Be aware of participants who have special dietary requirements and are not able to play the game. Ensure those participants are still included in the activity. For example, you could give them the role of team referee.

FOUNDATIONAL CONCEPT...RESILIENCE
Remember that resilience helps us rise above circumstances and adversity. Resilience enables us to face our challenges. How we meet the storms of life will determine the effect they have on others and ourselves.

Q. Do we look the storm in the face or do we run from it?

Being able to overcome adversity and challenges benefits not just us but everyone. Our story of challenge and triumph can give hope and strength to others in situations similar to ours. Resilience is for service.

In every situation, in every day, we make choices. As a result of these choices there are consequences. Consequences will either cause us to move forward in life, stop us from moving at all or cause us to move backwards. There are decisions that can fast-track us to our future and others that can keep us from it.

Decisions we make don't just affect our life, they also impact the people around us. Our choices can be selfish or selfless.

Every decision we make has a consequence. Often we don't realise that it's the small, everyday decisions that determine our destination.

PRESENTATION... RESPECT

RE·SPECT *[RI-SPEKT]* Esteem for or a sense of the worth or excellence of a person, the condition of being esteemed or honoured, to show regard or consideration for.

In an ideal world respect is something that we would extend to everyone. It is how we should act. Respect is something that shouldn't have to be earned, but given freely.

If we don't respect ourselves, it is difficult for us to respect others and others to respect us. Treat others the way you would like to be treated. When we respect ourselves, we tend not to willingly put ourselves in a position where we are disrespected. This is because we value ourselves. For example: because I respect myself, I will value my body by looking after it through regular exercise and healthy eating.

Respect can either be demanded or commanded. There is a big difference between the two. Demanding respect is where people may exert their dominance in a negative way. Commanding respect says much more about the person, not the position they may be given. People who command respect live in a way in which they don't need to demand anything. Their character speaks loudly to those around them; much louder than any title can demand. Who they are, not what they are or do, becomes what people respect.

We don't always get treated the way we should but we can choose to treat other people with respect.

ALL PEOPLE SHOULD RECEIVE RESPECT NO MATTER HOW DIFFERENT THEY ARE TO YOU.

GROUP DISCUSSION: RESPECT

Q. Name someone who you look up to and why. This person can be someone you know or a public figure.
Q. How can we respect ourselves?
Q. What does respect look like for you? How would you like people to show you respect?

(Starting off with these questions can help the participants understand each other more as well as help them see that how they want to be treated they need to treat others the same.)

Q. **How can we respect our friends, parents, family, and people from different cultures, religious, racial or linguistic backgrounds?** For example, not walking away when your parents are talking to you, listening to someone's story, or experiencing new food and traditions.

Q. **What are practical ways you can show respect to your fellow students and teachers?**
For example, listening, not speaking over each other, and speaking slowly and clearly to someone who has difficulty understanding English rather than speaking loudly to them.

ACTIVITY: THE LINE GAME

Mark a line on the floor with tape. Explain that when the facilitator makes a statement or asks a question, the participants need to stand on the line if it applies to them. If it doesn't apply to them, they are to stand off the line. To start the game, the facilitator is to ask questions or make statements that are general and then lead into more specific questions. Lead the specific questions or statements towards respect and bullying. The purpose of this activity is to remove individuals' sense of isolation around this topic and allow everyone to see that respect and bullying applies and impacts everyone in some capacity. Some examples include:

- Stand on the line if you play a sport
- Stay on the line if you've ever lost a game
- Stand on the line if you play an instrument or sing
- Stay on the line if you have ever made a mistake during a performance
- Stand on the line if you have ever had a bad day at school
- Stay on the line if you have had more than one bad day at school
- Stand on the line if you have ever been called names by someone
- Stay on the line if you have ever had someone try to pick a fight with you
- Stand on the line if you want bullying to stop.

DISCUSSION: BULLYING

Now that we have identified what respect looks like, what is the opposite of respecting someone? What does that look like?

Bullying is the opposite of respecting others.

Bullying involves intentional acts of harmful behaviour towards another person and normally occurs where there is a power imbalance i.e. where a more powerful person (or people) usurp themselves over another person that they see to be less than. These behaviours include:

- Name-calling
- Physically fighting
- Victimization through ignoring or isolating
- Intimidation and/or harassment, and
- Cyber-bullying

Bullying is not generally a single event of inappropriate behaviour between equals.

Q. A new student has arrived at your school halfway through Term 2. What could you do to help them feel included in a sports lesson?

Online bullying major challenge for today's students

Parents believe the top three challenges (extremely/very) for today's students are

Online bullying through social networks
60%

High pressure to do well in exams and assessments
51%

Life is more complicated, causing additional stress
49%

McCrindle (2019), Education Future Forum: Exploring rising parent engagement, the wellbeing focus and school complexity (used with permission).

RESEARCH AND RECORD CURRENT BULLYING STATISTICS RELEVANT TO YOUR GROUP

CYBER-BULLYING

It is much easier to be more outgoing or provocative online. People find they can be personally more aggressive and forward than they are in 'real-life' because they are hiding behind a computer screen or mobile phone. This can give people the false confidence to say or do things that they would not normally say face-to-face. What they are writing, posting or sending can have a significant negative impact on others.

DISCUSSION: CYBER-BULLYING

Q. What are some types of cyber-bullying?
Encourage the participants to come up with their thoughts. Then suggest some of the following forms if they have been left out. Forms of cyber-bullying include:

- Spreading rumours about people on social media, via text messages or online.
- Accessing another person's account information, without permission, to see their details or to pretend to be them.
- Sexting unsolicited photos or messages.
- Trolling

Q. What effect do you think cyber-bullying has on the recipient and the cyber-bullies?
Encourage the participants to come up with their thoughts. Then suggest some of the following forms if they have been left out:

- It can lead to depression and anxiety for the recipient.
- Once circulated on the internet, it may never disappear. Info and images can be found at later times.
- What is posted online may have a negative effect on future applications for college or employment.
- Cyber-bullies may face legal charges. e.g. if the cyber-bullying is sexual in nature such as sexting.

Q. What can you do to prevent cyber-bulling?
- Avoid getting involved in it yourself
- Avoid forwarding bullying texts and emails and exit online chat rooms
- Block the sender
- Ignore the message rather than respond in a manner that would encourage retaliation
- Think about how you can respond as a helpful bystander
- Request removal of objectionable websites.

SMALL GROUP DISCUSSION

> **Q. What can you do to display respect to yourself, your peers, and teachers or to your family this week?**

FOUNDATIONAL CONCEPT **THREE**

COURAGE

SESSION SIX TOO TRADITIONAL FOR TODAY.
SESSION SEVEN CAUSE & EFFECT.
SESSION EIGHT THE MAN FOR THE DREAM.

I HAVE A HOPE AND A FUTURE

INTRODUCTION

COUR·AGE *[KUR-IJ, KUHR-]* The quality of mind or spirit that enables a person to face difficulty; bravery. Courage gives us the ability to stand up for what is right.

CON·VIC·TION *[KUHN-VIK-SHUHN]* A fixed or firm, strong belief.

A conviction helps us make decisions, especially decisions that are important and significant. Convictions produce in us the ability to act with courage. Our convictions demonstrate what we value in life.

Fear is required for courage to exist. Courage can only be expressed in the company of fear. We can use our fears to exercise courage and through that, we can discover something within us that we didn't know we had.
Acting courageously highlights that we are not swayed by what other people will say or do about the decision or stand we are making.

COURAGE ALLOWS US TO NOT CONFORM TO THE NORM

Courage allows us to face our fears or opposition without backing down, acting on what is right. Courage can help us to identify healthy risks and face challenges that grow and stretch us. For example: the number 1 fear for many people is public speaking. Developing courage to address the fear of public speaking could allow a person to see that they may be gifted in that area. Courage helps us develop new skills and learn new things about us.

I HAVE A HOPE AND A FUTURE

6
COURAGE
SESSION SIX TOO TRADITIONAL FOR TODAY

RECOMMENDED LAYOUT

MATERIAL REQUIRED: Whiteboard & whiteboard markers; Paper; Pens/permanent markers/coloured pencils; Butcher's paper; Morse Code handout *(Appendix F)*.

ACTIVITY	DETAILS	NOTES/MATERIALS
ICEBREAKER 10 mins	**DISCUSSION** What Do You Look For?	
FOUNDATIONAL CONCEPT 10 mins	**COURAGE**	
PRESENTATION 35 mins	**GROUP DISCUSSION: TREATING OTHERS WELL** All groups will complete this activity regardless of whether Option 1 or Option 2 is chosen. **OPTION A:** • **ACTIVITY** Q & A with female guest • **GROUP DISCUSSION** Pornography **OPTION B:** • **ACTIVITY** Morse code	Paper, pens
SMALL GROUP DISCUSSION 5 mins	Q. What is one quality of a healthy relationship that is important to you? Q. How can you place value on a person in your world?	

NOTES

OUTCOMES
BY THE END OF THIS SESSION YOU WILL BE ABLE TO:
Develop understanding of a healthy relationship.
Explore how to treat person with respect and dignity.

ICEBREAKER
DISCUSSION: WHAT DO YOU LOOK FOR?

> Q. What do you think are the qualities that make a wonderful person?

FOUNDATIONAL CONCEPT

> Q. What are some examples that highlight someone being courageous?

COUR·AGE *[KUR-IJ, KUHR-]* The quality of mind or spirit that enables a person to face difficulty; bravery. Courage gives us the ability to stand up for what what is right.

CON·VIC·TION *[KUHN-VIK-SHUHN]* A fixed or firm, strong belief.
A conviction helps us make decisions, especially decisions that are important and significant. Convictions produce in us the ability to act with courage. Our convictions demonstrate what we value in life.

Fear is required for courage to exist. Courage can only be expressed in the company of fear. We can use our fears to exercise courage and through that, we can discover something within us that we didn't know we had.

Acting courageously highlights that we are not fearful of what other people will say or do about the decision or stand we are making. Courage allows us to not conform to the norm. Courage allows us to face our fears or opposition without backing down, acting on what is right.

PRESENTATION

GROUP DISCUSSION: TREATING OTHERS WELL

START WITH
Q. If it was your sister or mother being mistreated because of her gender, how would you respond and what type of life would you want for her? For example:

- Respect her at all times.
- Protect her dignity.
- Listen and be interested in her perspective.
- Speak to her and about her in a way that is always uplifting and never derogatory.

It is important to emphasise that every female shares a relationship with someone. They are someone's daughter, sister, and friend. They are more than an object for our eyes' attention.

IT TAKES COURAGE TO TREAT THE OPPOSITE SEX RIGHT, WITH RESPECT AND DIGNITY; PARTICULARLY WHEN PEOPLE AROUND US MAY WANT US TO DO THE OPPOSITE.

CONTINUE WITH '*What is an unhealthy relationship?*' Steve Biddulph in his book '*The New Manhood*' says:

"There are two common 'Hallmark' myths about relationships that need to be rectified. One is that people who love each other do not argue, that if you argue it means you have problems. Two is that the key to happiness is finding a compatible partner, if you find someone who likes what you like then everything will be fine. However both of these beliefs are untrue, healthy and happy couples argue especially in the early years, also compatibility is no guarantee of success. You can be very different people with different interests and still get along very well." Steve also adds, "Of course compatibility is nice, but its compatibility of values that matters most, not just liking the same music or football team! Being able to have conflicts, and solve them positively, is the most important sign of a good relationship."[23][sic]

FINISH WITH '*What is a healthy relationship?*' Note: It is important to focus on adolescent relationships rather than adult relationships.

---

[23] Biddulph, S 2010, *The New Manhood*, Finch Publishing, Sydney. Extracts from *The New Manhood: The handbook for a new kind of man* by Steve Biddulph are copyright of the author and are reproduced with the permission of Finch Publishing, Sydney.

This session's presentation section addresses the topic of pornography. Please consider the suitability of this topic before using this material with your program group (e.g. the age and maturity of the participants specific to your current STRENGTH program group, and any policies your organisation or hosting organisation may have applicable to the delivery of this content). Please select either the OPTION A or OPTION B activities for your specific program group.

Note: *Although the content of this program is copyright protected it does NOT constitute, or contain, legal, medical or other advice.*

OPTION A

ACTIVITY: Q & A WITH A FEMALE GUEST

Note: Don't bring your guest in until this point. Prior to this session, brief her on types of questions she might get asked. Think of the toughest questions the participants might ask so she can be prepared. Warn her that questions can be very sexually orientated and check whether she is prepared for this: she could find the questions quite offensive. It is important that the female guest answers the core foundation of the question rather than the question itself.

For example, "How can I get my girlfriend to have sex with me?" The female guest's response would be to suggest that this type of question is 'me orientated' and 'selfish'. The goal of sex is to please the other person, not to please you. This kind of guy is not the type of a guy a girl would want to be with.

Give each participant a piece of paper and ask them to write a question down that they have always wanted to ask a girl. Make sure it is emphasised to the group that every participant's question is to stay anonymous. Collect all the pieces of paper and place them in a hat/container. Emphasise and reinforce that the participants can't ask any question that is personally directed to the female guest. Questions have to be about females in general.

Have the guest pick one piece of paper at a time and read out the question and then give an answer. Make sure the male facilitator filters the questions, because there may be some odd, rude, or inappropriate ones. Do your best to answer all the questions.

In every group the questions asked by the participants will be different along with the issues that surface. Take initiative whilst facilitating this discussion and try to address issues as they arise.

PORNOGRAPHY
GROUP DISCUSSION: PORNOGRAPHY

INFORMATION

Pornography has the potential to rewire a person's brain, creating sexual desires and sexual functioning problems along with causing users to become preoccupied with sex. After growing accustomed to pornography, it can leave a person disappointed in their own sexual performance making them think something is wrong because they can't perform the way that porn stars do. It may be hard to enjoy sexual encounters with a partner and people may need to pull up pornographic images or replay porn scenes in their mind, which means the mind is elsewhere and not present in the moment with their partner.

Pornography aims to sexually arouse the person and involve them in a sexual relationship with it by giving a sexually stimulated and immediate gratifying experience. It's achieved by connecting the sight and sound of porn to the pleasure centres of a person's brain. As a result, the heart beats faster, breathing gets shallower and sexual organs throb, providing an instant arousal. When a person is sexually aroused, dopamine is released into our brain, producing a drug-like high. Adrenaline, endorphins and serotonin are also increased, overloading the brain with pleasurable chemicals. As a result, it strengthens the connection of pleasure with pornography and reduces the body's ability to release these pleasure chemicals under 'normal' life circumstances.

Pornography has a focus on power – feeling powerful and in control. Such concepts promote a self-focused approach to sex which can present problems in real-life relationships.

The average age for when a person will first view pornography is age 11 and the majority of 11-year-olds would not have any prior experience or knowledge of sex. Therefore what they see through pornography is what they believe sex to be like.

PORNOGRAPHY IMPACTS THE WAY WE THINK ABOUT WOMEN, SEXUALITY, INTIMACY AND ULTIMATELY WHAT A PERSON THINKS ABOUT THEIR OWN SEXUALITY.

Q. Why do people use pornography?
You may need to start this discussion as participants may hesitate to respond straight away. The aim is to facilitate discussion and explore the following reasons to see if any relate to the group.
Sometimes, people use porn to:
- Fit in with the crowd
- Escape from day-to-day life
- Find out what sex is like
- Experience pleasure, and
- Try something new

Q. Are there any issues around using pornography?
Through this discussion, explore how pornography can become an addiction that can carry through into adult life and how pornography affects the user and the people around them. Being exposed to pornography can create unrealistic expectations about what we think a real relationship is meant to be.

PORNOGRAPHY EXPOSES US TO A FANTASY WORLD WHICH IS NOT REALITY.

PORNOGRAPHY DOESN'T VALUE, RESPECT OR DIGNIFY OTHERS.

OPTION B

ACTIVITY: MORSE CODE

- Tell the participants a brief history of Morse code or show the group a short YouTube clip on this.
- Provide each participant with a Morse code worksheet *(see Appendix F)*.
- Have the participants divide into small groups and ask each group to work together to write the following words in Morse code (dots and dashes):

SIGNIFICANCE. RESILIENCE. COURAGE.

- Discuss the answers with the whole STRENGTH program group. You may choose to ask a small group to clap their response to one of the words and have the other groups identify which word they are clapping.
- Ask the participants if they know what the International Morse code distress signal is. *The correct response is SOS.*
- As a STRENGTH program group, clap the SOS Morse code sequence.

Note: *There are several versions of Morse code. If a participant knows a different version of Morse code explain that for today's activity the group will be using International Morse code.*

- Provide the participants with a piece of paper and pen then talk to them about how they can connect with adult support. For example, "It is really important that you have a trusted adult/grown-up that you can talk to about things that are important to you, including when you feel unsafe or when you need to send out an SOS. Take some time to think of a trusted adult you can talk to. If you cannot think of a person that is okay, I will write the names of people you can speak with on the board and everyone in the group can write down their details."

Note: *When providing contact names of a trusted adult the participants can speak to, only provide the details of professional counselling and support services e.g. the name and contact details of the school counsellor or youth helpline number. When running the program in a school, the school contact (e.g. the Principal) is to approve the contact people/organisations provided to the participants before the session commences.*

SMALL GROUP DISCUSSION

> Q. What is one quality of a healthy relationship that is important to you?
> Q. How can you place value on a person in your world? This does not have to be a partner. It can be a friend or family member.

I HAVE A HOPE AND A FUTURE

7

COURAGE
SESSION SEVEN CAUSE & EFFECT

RECOMMENDED LAYOUT

MATERIAL REQUIRED: TV series clip; Butcher's paper, paper; Pens/coloured pencils/permanent markers; Timer for icebreaker game; Whiteboard markers & whiteboard; Cause & effect scenarios handout *(Appendix G)*.

ACTIVITY	DETAILS	NOTES/MATERIALS
ICEBREAKER 10 mins	**ACTIVITY** Pictionary	Paper, pens/coloured pencils/permanent markers
FOUNDATIONAL CONCEPT 10 mins	**COURAGEOUS**	
PRESENTATION 35 mins	Cause & Effect **GROUP DISCUSSION** Risk-taking **GROUP ACTIVITY** Healthy & Unhealthy Risk-taking **GROUP ACTIVITY** Cause & Effect Scenarios	Paper, pens, Cause & Effect Scenarios handout
SMALL GROUP DISCUSSION 5 mins	Q. What is some healthy risk-taking that you would like to explore? What do you think you will achieve from actioning this?	
FITNESS AND HEALTHY EATING 10 mins	**HEALTHY EATING** **FITNESS ACTIVITIES**	Facilitator may need to bring in some food items.

NOTES

OUTCOMES
BY THE END OF THIS SESSION YOU WILL BE ABLE TO:
Gain understanding of the difference between healthy and unhealthy risk-taking.
Identify consequences to healthy and unhealthy risk-taking.

ICEBREAKER
ACTIVITY: PICTIONARY
Split the group up into their teams and play a few games of Pictionary. Observe how each team member interacts with the drawer. Highlight your observations at the end of the game, particularly about what worked well.

FOUNDATIONAL CONCEPT
COUR·AGE *[KUR-IJ, KUHR-]* The quality of mind or spirit that enables a person to face difficulty; bravery. Courage gives us the ability to stand up for what is right. We need convictions to identify what it is we stand for.

CON·VIC·TION *[KUHN-VIK-SHUHN]* A fixed or firm, strong belief.
A conviction helps us make decisions, especially decisions that are important and significant. Convictions produce in us the ability to act with courage. Our convictions demonstrate what we value in life.

Fear is required for courage to exist. Courage can only be expressed in the company of fear. We can use our fears to exercise courage and through that, we can discover something within us that we didn't know we had.

Acting courageously highlights that we are not swayed by what other people will say or do about the decision or stand we are making. Courage allows us to not conform to the norm. Courage allows us to face our fears or opposition without backing down, acting on what is right.

Courage can help us to identify healthy risks and face challenges that grow and stretch us. For example: the number 1 fear for many people is public speaking. Developing courage to address the fear of public speaking could allow a person to see that they may be gifted in that area.

> Q. What do you think are risk-taking activities/sports?
> Q. What is about these activities that people find attractive?

PRESENTATION
CAUSE & EFFECT
Young people can love to push the boundaries, take risks and be impulsive. Why?

They tend to take risks because their emotional and cognitive (decision-making) development has not fully matured yet. This limits their ability to make healthy decisions. Adolescents are more inclined to make impulsive decisions based on what makes them feel good and what makes them fit in to what their peers are doing, without considering the consequences of the decisions or whether it is the right decision.

GROUP DISCUSSION: RISK-TAKING

> Q. Why should we take risks in life?
> Q. What are the benefits of taking risks?

Some forms of risk-taking can be healthy; it can move us out of our comfort zones, reveal to us what we are capable of and what is within us. Sometimes we can make life too safe and not take any risks, and other times we take unhealthy risks. It's important to work out what risk-taking is healthy and unhealthy.

Sometimes people are too scared to take risks for various reasons such as fear of failure and what people will think of them if they fail; they don't believe they can succeed. Fear of failure cannot be a good enough reason not to try. Courage is required to take healthy risks.

GROUP ACTIVITY: HEALTHY & UNHEALTHY RISK-TAKING
What types of risks have benefits and what types of risks can have serious negative consequences? Split up into teams and come up with as many suggestions in 5 mins.

Unhealthy risk-taking is where you or others are in a position/situation which is unsafe, or your life or others' lives/health are at risk or in danger. Our minds might think we are in control but our behaviour shows we aren't e.g. drink driving.

GROUP ACTIVITY: CAUSE & EFFECT SCENARIOS

This activity shows how someone's behaviour can impact another person's life, which in turn could impact many other people's lives.

Below are scenarios that are possible circumstances which young people experience. As the facilitator, ensure that these scenarios come to life, don't just read them out. You can make them come alive through explaining them in an expressive manner that engages the group. *(See Appendix G.)*

Explore in teams all the possible outcomes that could realistically happen as a result of the following scenarios. Encourage the teams to come up with short-term as well as long-term effects on the wider community, not just the people involved in the scenario.

EXAMPLE 1: DRINK DRIVING Simon goes to his friend's BBQ on Saturday afternoon. He enjoys having beers with his mates and watching the football. Simon and his friends are involved in a mini drinking competition to see who can drink the most beers throughout the afternoon. When the BBQ is over, Simon thinks he is fine to drive home and gets behind the wheel. On driving home, he is unable to control the car and hits a bus stop where a child has been waiting for the next bus. The child has been hurt in the accident.

EXAMPLE 2: DRUGS AND ALCOHOL Tyson has just moved schools and really wants to fit in and make good friends. It's Friday night and one of the guys invites him to hang out at the local park where they regularly go. When Tyson arrives they are all taking drugs and offer him some. Tyson takes the drugs because he wants to be accepted by the group.

EXAMPLE 3: BULLYING A group of guys have been enjoying picking on a girl in their grade by constantly calling her names because she is overweight. She goes home many times after school crying and refuses to eat in front of people. She is always putting herself down in front of others.

EXAMPLE 4: RISK-TAKING BEHAVIOUR Justin has just got his learner's license and he considers himself to be a really good driver. His friend needs a lift somewhere urgently and begs Justin to drive him. Justin's parents are not home and he has access to their car.

As the facilitator, it's important to be aware that some of these scenarios or topics discussed could be a concern for some participants. Write up some professional support services on the board or as a handout for the group to contact. e.g. a youth hotline number, the contact details of the school counsellor. Where needed make an appropriate referral e.g. to the classroom teacher.

> **Q. Why do we have boundaries?**
> Boundaries are there to stop us from hurting ourselves or others. They keep us safe and can protect us. Boundaries create security, freedom and provide direction. What is the effect of having no boundaries? We can go out of control. Illustrate this topic by explaining how a race car races on a track that has barricades around the track. The barricades are there to make sure that if the car goes off the track, any harm done to the car and driver is minimised by the barricades. Barricades are like a boundary. Without the barricades, the car can fly into the crowd and hurt more people than just the driver, or the car could roll down a ditch causing a lot of damage to the driver and the car. This example illustrates that boundaries on a race track are there to keep the driver safe and protect the car from causing extensive damage to its external environment.

SMALL GROUP DISCUSSION

Q. What is some healthy risk-taking that you would like to explore?
Q. What do you think you will achieve from actioning this?

NOTE TO FACILITATOR //
Below are some ideas for getting active. Choose a range of activities you like or think you might like to try [31]:
- Play a team sport. It is a great way to spend time with your friends or make new ones.
- Limit the time you spend watching television, on social media or playing video games.
- Walk, run or cycle to where you need to go.
- Try something new like surfing, tennis or training for a triathlon.

---

[31] Taken from Department of Health and Ageing, *Get Out and Get Active brochure.*

HEALTHY LIFESTYLE CHOICES
FITNESS AND HEALTHY EATING

HEALTHY EATING: ACTIVITY

Arrange some food items on the table and ask the group to put them into the healthy section or not healthy section. Such food items can include: fruit, vegetables, chocolate, chips, popcorn, fizzy drinks, juice, milk, cereals.

Note: For this activity, it is recommended that you bring in some food items; however, if you do not want to bring in food items you could use pictures of food instead.

INFORMATION An eating pattern that contains a healthy variety of foods such as vegetables (including legumes, i.e. peas, beans and lentils), fruit and cereals, and is low in fat, salt and sugar, will help you to be at your healthy best. A healthy diet can help you have the energy, strength and good health to try new active challenges. If you combine healthy eating and physical activity, it will also help you maintain a healthy weight *(for more information on healthy eating visit www.healthyactive.gov.au).*

> **FITNESS: GROUP DISCUSSION**
> Q. What things can you do to maintain a healthy lifestyle?
> Q. What are the benefits of being active?

INFORMATION It is recommended that young people participate in at least 60 minutes of exercise every day. Being active is good for you in so many ways. It can provide a huge range of fun experiences, help you feel good, and improve your health.

Discuss some of the benefits of being active. Here are some examples:
Having fun with friends and making new ones. Opportunity for new skills and challenges. Boost of confidence. Improved fitness. Bones and muscle mass get stronger. Improved posture. Maintenance of healthy weight. Improved health of your heart. Helps you relax and reduce stress.

> **Q. What type of fun activities can you take part in?** Games. Sports. Having fun with friends. Getting places (walking, cycling and skateboarding). School or family activities.

NOTES

I HAVE A HOPE AND A FUTURE

COURAGE

SESSION EIGHT THE MAN FOR THE DREAM

RECOMMENDED LAYOUT

MATERIAL REQUIRED: Whiteboard markers and whiteboard; What Would You Do? handout *(Appendix I)*; Imagine handout *(Appendix J)*; Goal Setting Timeline handout *(Appendix K)*; Understanding Your Opposition handout *(Appendix L)*; Pens/coloured pencils/permanent markers; Paper.

ACTIVITY	DETAILS	NOTES/MATERIALS
ICEBREAKER 10 mins	**ACTIVITY** Passions & Likes	
FOUNDATIONAL CONCEPT 10 mins	**COURAGE** "What is Your Life's Blueprint?"	
PRESENTATION 35 mins	**ACTIVITY** What Would You Do/Create with $1M? **ACTIVITY** Mind Mapping **ACTIVITY** Guest Speaker **ACTIVITY** Identify and Action a Dream or Goal **DISCUSSION** Dream Storming	Pens/ coloured pencils/ permanent markers, paper, What Would You Do? handout, Imagine handout, Goal Setting Timeline handout, Understanding Your Opposition handout
SMALL GROUP DISCUSSION 5 mins	Q. What positive quality do you have or would like to develop that can help you to achieve your goals and dreams?	

NOTES

OUTCOMES
BY THE END OF THIS SESSION YOU WILL BE ABLE TO:
Recognise the importance of goal setting to achieve a dream or goal.

ICEBREAKER
ACTIVITY: PASSIONS AND DISLIKES
Go around the group and ask participants to share what they are most passionate about. If someone is unsure about what they are most passionate about, ask them to tell the group about an activity that they like participating in.

FOUNDATIONAL CONCEPT
REITERATE THE FOUNDATIONAL CONCEPT OF COURAGE: COUR·AGE [KUR-IJ, KUHR-]
The quality of mind or spirit that enables a person to face difficulty; bravery.

Every individual was created for a purpose in a specific time in history. Everyone has a sense of purpose attached to their life. No one was created by mistake. Everyone has a reason for their existence. It is up to us to find out that reason or purpose for our existence.

No matter what we do in life, we can live with an understanding that we are made for a purpose.

Fear is required for courage to exist. Courage can only be expressed in the company of fear. We can use our fears to exercise courage and through that, we can discover something within us that we didn't know we had.

Acting courageously highlights that we are not swayed by what other people will say or do about the decision or stand we are making. Courage allows us to not conform to the norm. Courage allows us to face our fears or opposition without backing down, acting on what is right.

Courage can help us to identify healthy risks and face challenges that grow and stretch us. For example: the number 1 fear for many people is public speaking. Developing courage to address the fear of public speaking could allow a person to see that they may be gifted in that area. Courage helps us develop new skills and learn new things about ourselves.

FEAR OF FAILURE CANNOT BE A GOOD ENOUGH REASON NOT TO TRY.

PRESENTATION
"AM I THE MAN I NEED TO BE TO REALISE THE DREAM THAT I SEE?" // JUDAH SMITH

Explore this with the group.
A person's work or career can be centred on things that they enjoy in life. Work life does not have to be a drag. Everyone has gifts and talents that can be developed to become their strengths. Discovering and developing our gifts and talents can be the key to positively impacting our communities.

ACTIVITY: WHAT WOULD YOU DO/CREATE WITH $1M?
Tell the group you want them to think about something they may never have thought about before. If you were to give each of them $1M to come up with a business idea and to create a company, what kind of company would they create? They will need to return the $1M back to you in 10 years time. Encourage them to think about what they would spend the $1M on and how they could grow their business. *(See Appendix I.)*

Some will come up with really creative, pioneering companies. Commend them on their creativity and emphasise that they could actually do that.

Share stories of people who have started successful businesses out of nothing. Encourage the participants not to wait for someone to give them $1M to start the business they are capable of taking small steps to create now.

HIGHLIGHT: People who come up with great business ideas often start with a small amount or no money.

ACTIVITY: MIND MAPPING
Split into pairs or teams and then discuss as a group:

Q. What difference would I like to make in the world?
Q. Whose lives do I hope to positively impact and how?
Q. What type of person would I like to be?

ACTIVITY: GUEST SPEAKER
This is a great session to bring in a guest that will inspire the participants about their future. The ideal guest is someone who is in an industry that the participants are interested in. For example it might be a pro skater, pro football player, mechanic and so forth.

Introduce your guest and ask them to share about their job including why they decided to go down that path, what they love about their job, what is challenging about their job, what they have personally learnt about themselves through their work, and what they had to leave behind to get where they are today. Ask them to share what they are passionate about and how it links into their day-to-day job.

Encourage the participants to ask your guest any questions they might have about their particular career.

Ask your guest to explain the stages and steps it took them to get where they are today. What were they doing at the participants' ages to work towards their goal? The aim of this discussion is to help the participants understand that they may have to take many small steps over a number of years to achieve their goals. What can the participants start to do TODAY to work towards their goals. *(See Appendix J.)*

ACTIVITY: IDENTIFY AND ACTION A DREAM OR GOAL
Use the handout IMAGINE for ideas. (See Appendix K.)

Ask the participants to write down on a piece of paper possible short, medium and long term goals that they can work towards. Be mindful that some participants will not write anything because they may be unsure what their goals are.

Use two or three examples from what a few participants have written down to explore on the board together as a group some practical steps on how they could get there. For example, if someone wants to be a mechanic, discuss as a group what they need to do to become a mechanic. Some suggestions are: doing work experience in a mechanic shop, complete an education pathway, enrol in a mechanic course and so forth.

Make sure you emphasise the importance of goal setting and setting realistic goals that the participants can achieve NOW, and outline the future steps/goals they will need to take as well.

For the participants that are unsure about what they want to do with their life, include them in this group process either by using a career that they might be interested in or encouraging them to suggest steps to take to achieve that career.

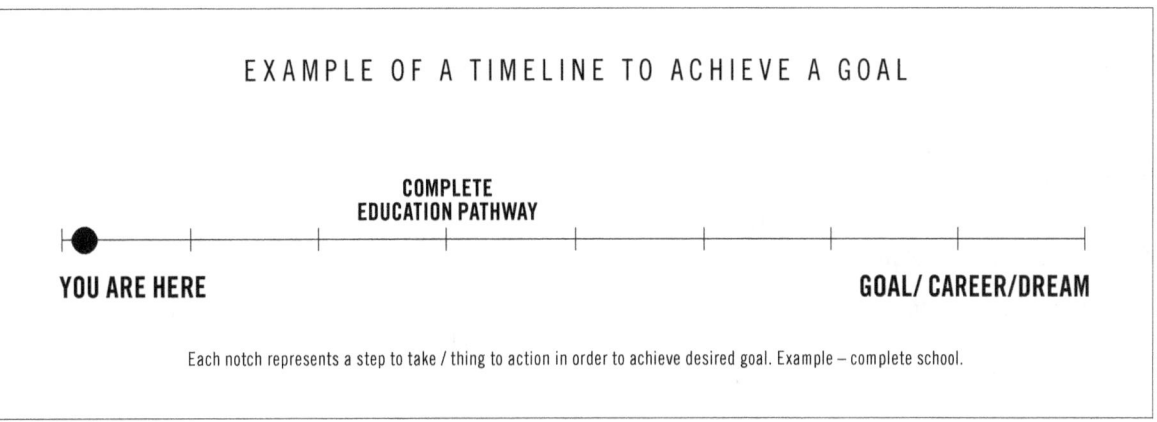

Your team is who and what will help you to achieve your goals and dreams. Your opposition are the things that could stop you achieving your goals and dreams. *(See Appendix L.)*

YOUR TEAM	YOUR OPPOSITION
1.	1.
2.	2.
3.	3.
4.	4.
5.	5.

STEP 1 Recognise what is in front of you. Understand the opposition before you run on the field.
STEP 2 Identify how to side step, avoid or dodge the opposition
STEP 3 What are the strengths and weakness of the opposition?
STEP 4 Who is on your team — which friends can keep you on your path?

Explore possible goals that are relevant to the group. An example of a goal is to join a rep sports team. Explore this concept through identifying who is on your team and things that could be opposition when it comes to training for the team. Now, complete the table for that situation.

YOUR TEAM	YOUR OPPOSITION
1.	1.
2.	2.
3.	3.
4.	4.
5.	5.

DISCUSSION: DREAM STORMING

Q. There are certain character traits and qualities we need to help us achieve our dreams. What do you think these could be?

- Hard work
- Respect
- Working together (you never know who you will meet that will help you get to where you want to go)
- Initiative/trying new things
- Confidence

Ask your guest to share how they developed certain qualities to help them become resilient to achieve their goals.

"IN-BETWEEN A DREAM AND REALITY IS HARD WORK" //AUTHOR UNKNOWN

SMALL GROUP DISCUSSION

Q. What positive quality do you have or would like to develop that can help you to achieve your goals and dreams?

I HAVE A HOPE AND A FUTURE

9
COURAGE
SESSION NINE LIVE THE ADVENTURE

RECOMMENDED LAYOUT

MATERIAL REQUIRED: STRENGTH Graduation Certificates *(Appendix M)*

ACTIVITY	DETAILS	NOTES/MATERIALS
PRESENTATION Variable timing	**GROUP ACTIVITY OR EXCURSION**	
SMALL GROUP DISCUSSION Variable timing	- Encourage each participant to share what he has learnt from the program	STRENGTH Graduation Certificates

NOTES

OUTCOMES
BY THE END OF THIS SESSION YOU WILL BE ABLE TO:
Describe what he has learnt from the program.
Participate in a team-building activity.

PRESENTATION
Plan in advance to take the group on an excursion that will allow them to implement some of the teamwork skills they have learnt during their time on the STRENGTH program. e.g. a rock climbing activity.

On the way to the excursion, talk to the participants about what they are going to do. Build up expectation and get them prepared. Incorporate what the STRENGTH sessions have covered that relates to this activity. For example, they will have the opportunity to increase their resilience by not giving up even though the activity might get hard.

If you are unable to take the group offsite, come up with other activities that will build teamwork and create a sense of accomplishment amongst the group. Suggestions may include sports activities on school grounds.

Here are some things for you to consider and organise in order to make this outing a success.

TRANSPORT	Chartered bus, public transport or choose a location within walking distance.
PERMISSIONS	A school authorisation to take the participants off school grounds. Where an activity is run with students from a school, a school staff member(s) will normally be required to lead the excursion.
	Parental authorisation (permission notes need to be made up and distributed by the school contact; ask a teacher for guidelines as to what information is required on the note, however, the school usually organises this).
	A school authorisation for extra time (this outing might require more time than one school period).
COST	Try and keep the cost for each individual under $10.

SMALL GROUP DISCUSSION
Encourage each participant to share what he has learnt from the program and hand each participant their STRENGTH Graduation Certificate.

NOTES

APPENDICES

APPENDIX A: Strict Rules Game
APPENDIX B: Number Plate
APPENDIX C: Friendship Quiz
APPENDIX D: Personal Reflections
APPENDIX E: Feeling Cards
APPENDIX F: Morse Code
APPENDIX G: Scenarios
APPENDIX I: What Would You Do?
APPENDIX J: Goal Setting Timeline
APPENDIX K: Imagine
APPENDIX L: Understanding Your Opposition
APPENDIX M: STRENGTH Graduation Certificate

APPENDIX A: STRICT RULES GAME

GROUP RULES

No talking at all.
Sit up straight with your hands on the desk at all times.
Everyone look to the front of the classroom.
No making noise at anytime.
Uniforms need to be well presented at all times.
Shoes need to be polished.

GROUP RULES

No talking at all.
Sit up straight with your hands on the desk at all times.
Everyone look to the front of the classroom.
No making noise at anytime.
Uniforms need to be well presented at all times.
Shoes need to be polished.

GROUP RULES

No talking at all.
Sit up straight with your hands on the desk at all times.
Everyone look to the front of the classroom.
No making noise at anytime.
Uniforms need to be well presented at all times.
Shoes need to be polished.

GROUP RULES

No talking at all.
Sit up straight with your hands on the desk at all times.
Everyone look to the front of the classroom.
No making noise at anytime.
Uniforms need to be well presented at all times.
Shoes need to be polished.

APPENDIX B: NUMBER PLATE

MY NUMBER PLATE

MY NUMBER PLATE

MY NUMBER PLATE

APPENDIX C: FRIENDSHIP QUIZ – 1/2

TICK HOW YOU WOULD RESPOND TO THE FOLLOWING SITUATIONS:

1. A kid in your class has been having a hard time with some guys in your grade who are picking on him. What do you do?

- ☐ Sit back and watch them bully him. You're glad it's not you.
- ☐ Stand up for him and report it to the teacher.
- ☐ Befriend him and invite him into your circle of friends.

2. Your friend is a star football player. He is regarded by his peers as someone everyone wants to be like. Colleges are coming to your school to scout players they can offer scholarships to. He has told you that he will be taking steroids so he can look bigger and stand out to the scouts. What do you?

- ☐ Talk him out of it by giving advice on the health risks and what could happen if he gets caught (he could get drug tested, lose his reputation and not be offered a place at college.)
- ☐ Tell him to go for it. It's worth taking the risk, and you don't want him to succeed.
- ☐ Don't say anything; it's his free choice.
- ☐ Tell someone because it's illegal.

3. Your friend is going through a hard time. After a bad day, he tells you he wants to drink alcohol to forget about his problems. What do you do?

- ☐ Join him. Any excuse to drink is great for you.
- ☐ Offer an alternative activity you could do together that would cheer him up. You know that drinking is not really going to help him deal with his problems.

APPENDIX C: FRIENDSHIP QUIZ – 2/2

4. Your friend has told you he's being beaten up at school but he doesn't want you to tell anyone. What do you do?

☐ Say nothing. You respect your friend's decision even though you're concerned about him.

☐ Report it to the teacher or trusted adult who you think can help him.

☐ Tell a friend.

5. You have formed friendships with a great crew of guys. They always have your back and never pay you out. You are out with your friends on the weekend hanging out at the local shops. Your friends see this guy walking past who they don't like and start beating him up. You pull back as you don't want to be a part of it. Your friends tell you that you have to be involved and if you want them to be loyal to you, you have to be loyal to them. What do you do?

☐ Get involved in the fight, you don't want them to come after you next time.

☐ Tell them you don't agree with this and walk away.

☐ Report it to someone in authority.

APPENDIX D: PERSONAL REFLECTIONS

LIST OF POSITIVE ACHIEVEMENTS I HAVE ACCOMPLISHED

1. _____
2. _____
3. _____
4. _____
5. _____
6. _____
7. _____
8. _____

LIST OF DIFFICULT SITUATIONS I HAVE OVERCOME

1. _____
2. _____
3. _____
4. _____
5. _____
6. _____
7. _____
8. _____

APPENDIX E: FEELING CARDS

ANGRY
STRENGTH
SIGNIFICANCE. RESILIENCE. COURAGE.

HAPPY
STRENGTH
SIGNIFICANCE. RESILIENCE. COURAGE.

SAD
STRENGTH
SIGNIFICANCE. RESILIENCE. COURAGE.

FEARFUL
STRENGTH
SIGNIFICANCE. RESILIENCE. COURAGE.

COMBINATION
STRENGTH
SIGNIFICANCE. RESILIENCE. COURAGE.

APPENDIX E: FEELING CARDS

FURIOUS
STRENGTH

IRRITATED
STRENGTH

ANNOYED
STRENGTH

TICKED OFF
STRENGTH

HUMILIATED
STRENGTH

APPENDIX E: FEELING CARDS

FRUSTRATED
STRENGTH

HURT
STRENGTH

SARCASTIC
STRENGTH

DISGUSTED
STRENGTH

APPENDIX E: FEELING CARDS

EXCITED
STRENGTH

SATISFIED
STRENGTH

PLEASED
STRENGTH

JOYFUL
STRENGTH

DELIGHTED
STRENGTH

APPENDIX E: FEELING CARDS

COMFORTABLE
STRENGTH
SIGNIFICANCE. RESILIENCE. COURAGE.

HOPEFUL
STRENGTH
SIGNIFICANCE. RESILIENCE. COURAGE.

SURPRISED
STRENGTH
SIGNIFICANCE. RESILIENCE. COURAGE.

POSITIVE
STRENGTH
SIGNIFICANCE. RESILIENCE. COURAGE.

APPENDIX E: FEELING CARDS

GRIEF — STRENGTH
MISERABLE — STRENGTH
DOWN — STRENGTH
DISAPPOINTED — STRENGTH
HURT — STRENGTH

APPENDIX E: FEELING CARDS

LONELY
STRENGTH

FORGOTTEN
STRENGTH

REMORSEFUL
STRENGTH

REJECTED
STRENGTH

APPENDIX E: FEELING CARDS

NERVOUS
STRENGTH

TERRIFIED
STRENGTH

ANXIOUS
STRENGTH

WORRIED
STRENGTH

CONCERNED
STRENGTH

APPENDIX E: FEELING CARDS

AFRAID
STRENGTH

UNCERTAIN
STRENGTH

OUT OF CONTROL
STRENGTH

UNEASY
STRENGTH

APPENDIX E: FEELING CARDS

GUILTY
STRENGTH

JEALOUS
STRENGTH

SHAME
STRENGTH

EMBARRASSED
STRENGTH

UNCOMFORTABLE
STRENGTH

APPENDIX E: FEELING CARDS

CONFUSED   STRENGTH
TORN   STRENGTH
ENVIOUS   STRENGTH
COMPASSION   STRENGTH

[APPENDICES] **143**

APPENDIX F: MORSE CODE

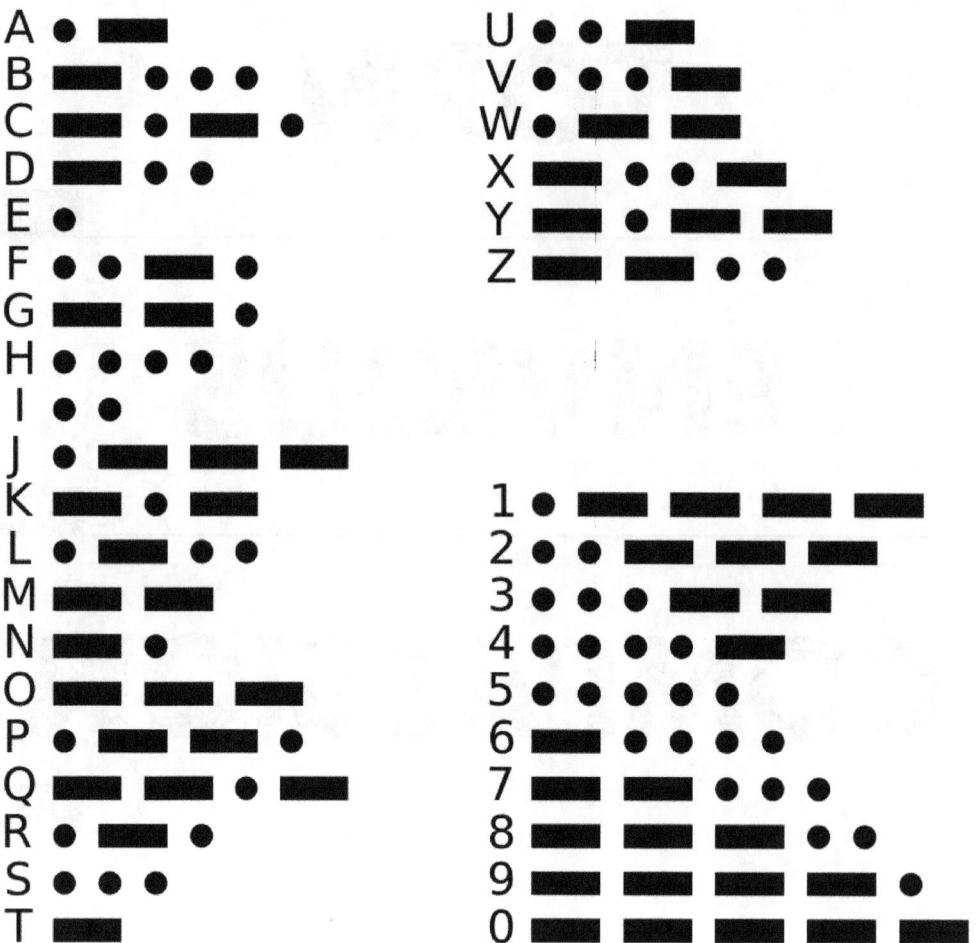

APPENDIX G: SCENARIOS

EXAMPLE 1: DRINK DRIVING Simon goes to his friend's BBQ on Saturday afternoon. He enjoys having beers with his mates and watching the football. Simon and his friends are involved in a mini drinking competition to see who can drink the most beers throughout the afternoon. When the BBQ is over, Simon thinks he is fine to drive home and gets behind the wheel. On driving home, he is unable to control the car and hits a bus stop where a child has been waiting for the next bus. The child has been hurt in the accident.

EXAMPLE 2: DRUGS AND ALCOHOL Tyson has just moved schools and really wants to fit in and meet good friends. It's Friday night and one of the guys invites him to hang out at the local park where they regularly go. When Tyson arrives, they are all taking drugs and offer him some. Tyson takes the drugs because he wants to be accepted by the group.

EXAMPLE 3: BULLYING A group of guys have been enjoying picking on a girl in their grade by constantly calling her names because she is overweight. She goes home many times after school crying and refuses to eat in front of people. She is always putting herself down in front of others.

EXAMPLE 4: RISK-TAKING BEHAVIOUR Justin has just got his learner's license and he considers himself to be a really good driver. His friend really needs a lift somewhere urgently and begs Justin to drive him. Justin's parents are not home and he has access to their car.

APPENDIX I: WHAT WOULD YOU DO?

WHAT WOULD YOU DO/CREATE WITH $1M?

_____
_____
_____
_____
_____
_____
_____

WHAT WOULD YOU DO/CREATE WITH $1M?

_____
_____
_____
_____
_____
_____
_____

APPENDIX J: GOAL SETTING TIMELINE

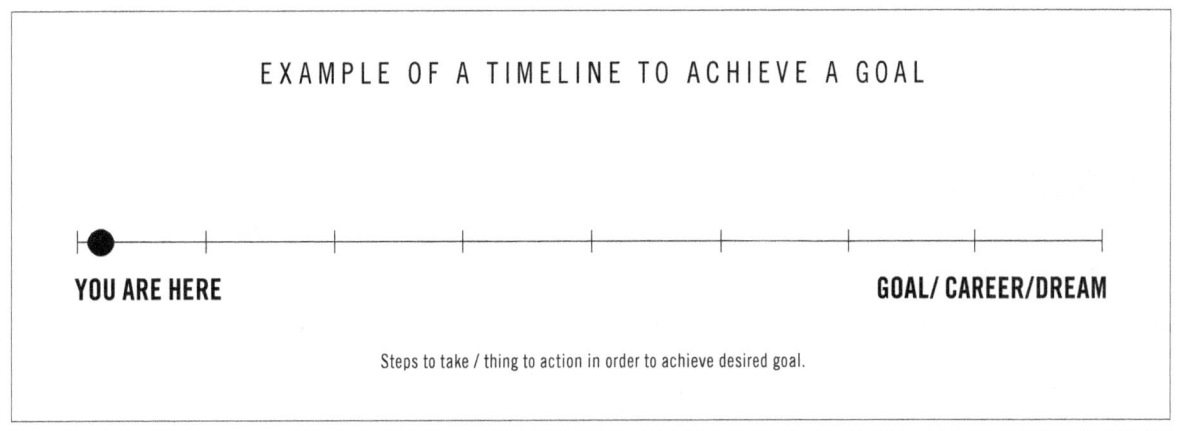

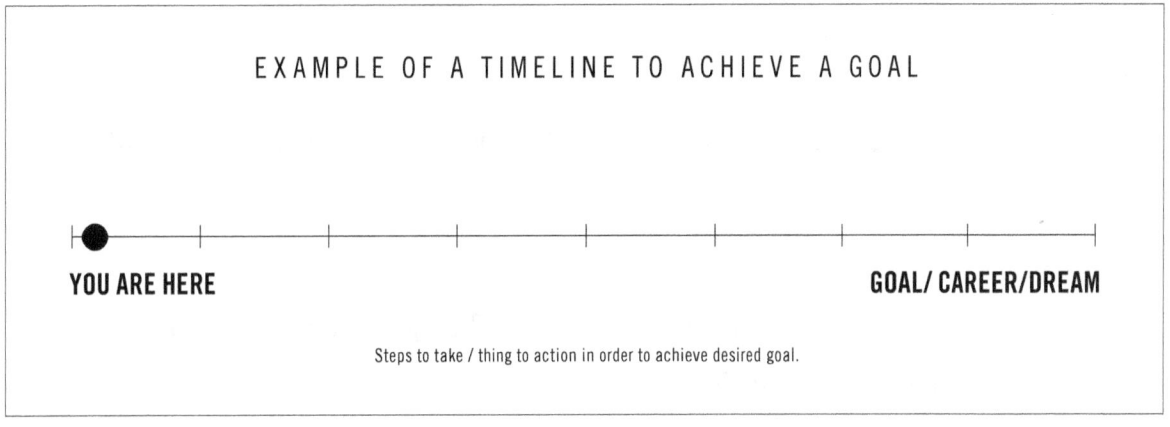

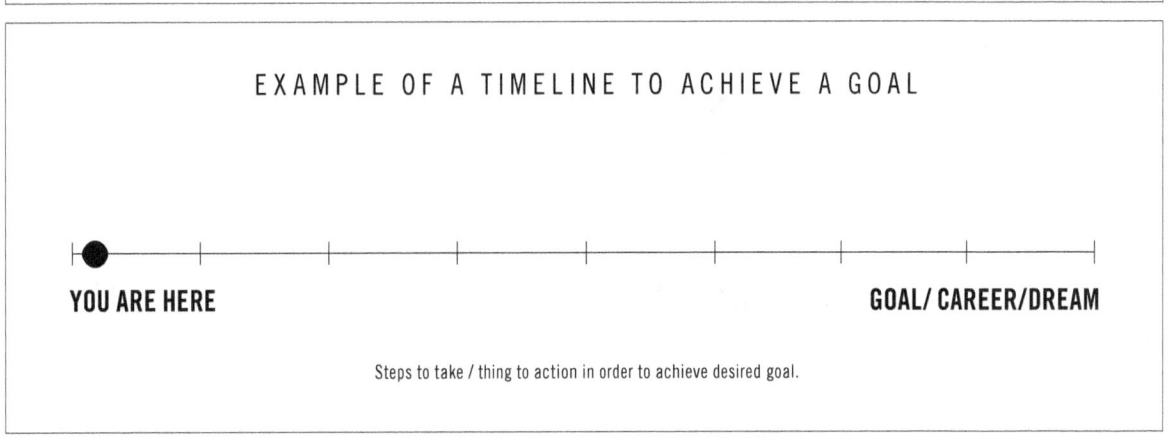

[APPENDICES] **147**

APPENDIX K: IMAGINE
[USE THIS HANDOUT FOR IDEAS ON GOAL SETTING]

IMAGINE

BIRTHDAY SPEECHES
Imagine it is your birthday. What would you like people to say about you for your birthday speech? What would you like people to write about you on your birthday card?

LIKES
If you had the total approval and admiration of everyone, regardless of what you do, what would you do with your life?

ROLE MODELS
What role models do you look up to? Who inspires you? What personal strengths or qualities do they have that you admire?

CHARACTER STRENGTHS
What personal strengths and qualities do you already have? Which ones would you like to develop? How would you like to apply them?

WEALTH
Imagine you win the lottery or inherit a fortune. How would you spend it? Who would you share it with?

APPENDIX L: UNDERSTANDING YOUR OPPOSITION

YOUR TEAM
1. _____
2. _____
3. _____
4. _____
5. _____

YOUR OPPOSITION
1. _____
2. _____
3. _____
4. _____
5. _____

YOUR TEAM
1. _____
2. _____
3. _____
4. _____
5. _____

YOUR OPPOSITION
1. _____
2. _____
3. _____
4. _____
5. _____

YOUR TEAM
1. _____
2. _____
3. _____
4. _____
5. _____

YOUR OPPOSITION
1. _____
2. _____
3. _____
4. _____
5. _____

APPENDIX M: STRENGTH GRADUATION CERTIFICATE

CERTIFICATE OF ACHIEVEMENT

[TO RECOGNISE]

_____

FOR SUCCESSFULLY COMPLETING

STRENGTH
SIGNIFICANCE. RESILIENCE. COURAGE.

_____
DATE

_____
STRENGTH FACILITATOR

_____
STRENGTH CO-FACILITATOR